A Travellers' Guide to Wild Flowers of Newfoundland

Canada

Bill & June Titford

Flora Frames
1995

i

Flora Frames
P.O. Box 28141
St. John's, NF A1B 4J8
Canada

Layout and design by:
MosCraft Design and VideoWorks
Paradise, NF

Canadian Cataloguing in Publication Data

Titford, Bill, 1933 –

A Travellers' Guide to Wildflowers of Newfoundland, Canada

Includes bibliographical references and index.
ISBN 0-9699459-0-6

1. Wildflowers – Newfoundland – Identification.
2. Wildflowers – Newfoundland – Pictorial works.
1 Titford, June, 1935 –   II. Title

QK203.N4T47 1995   582.13'09718   C95-950105-3
Printed in Hong Kong

Cover:
Small trap skiffs, used by fishermen in the in-shore fishery, swing gently on their collars on a bright Sunday morning at Tors Cove while sea gulls wheel and wait for the following week's activities to begin. On the horizon beyond the wharf is Green Island, a sea-bird sanctuary. Tors Cove is one of many quiet, scenic communities along the Southern Shore Highway leading southwards from St. John's.

The three flowers shown on the cover, from left to right, are:
Tansy Ragwort (Senecio jacobaea) – See page 59.
Small Purple Fringed Orchid (Habenaria psycodes) – See page 77.
Bogbean (Menyanthes trifoliata) – See page 43.

This book is dedicated
to the memory of
Bill's mother and father,
Vera and Billie,
and our daughter,
Jane.

May it inspire an increased appreciation
of beauty in the world around us.

Acknowledgements

W e wish to thank Dr. Peter J. Scott, Curator, Agnes Marion Ayre Herbarium, Memorial University of Newfoundland, for help so willingly given in species recognition from photographs. Thanks also to the staff of Dr. A. C. Hunter Library for the ready availability of botanical references, and most especially, for maintaining a quiet, reflective reading environment which contributed greatly to the completion of this book.

Gathering and identifying these photographs has been a labour of love for the natural beauty of our Province. The authors have diligently researched the proper identification of each flower and regret any errors contained herein.

A Shared Horizon

Like root and flower, leaf and stem,
People and beast we mimic them.
From seed paternal and maternal
We rise as though a seedling vernal.
Body and mind are fore-ordained
As we to ancestry are chained.

Constrained within our earthly bower,
Our fetters looser than the flower,
We choose with whom to share our seed
And choose the soil on which to breed.
We nurture and inspire our young
On paths from which our genes have sprung.

Yet still we know so little of
Capacity for hate and love,
And many a countless other trait
That in our being dormant wait
To be released for good or ill
Dependent on a strength of will.

We strive to know our purpose here
And feel we have a cross to bear.
We strive to build upon the past,
But feel, withal, the die is cast.
We put our faith in ghosts sublime
To lead us to the end of time.

So too the flora of this earth
Strives to improve its sense of worth.
Through normal and abnormal twist
It rose from out primordial mist.
Now gene to gene with us it stands
And moves with us to foreign lands.

United in the earth's embrace,
Yet seeking still a sense of place
Within a universal scheme
The culmination of a dream,
To found an Eden, if we can,
Together – plant and beast and man.

W.B.T.

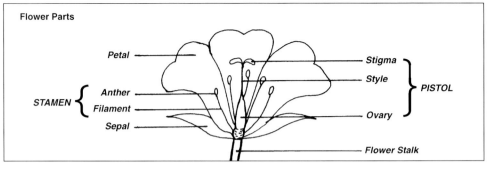

Flower Parts

Petal
Anther
STAMEN
Filament
Sepal
Stigma
Style
PISTOL
Ovary
Flower Stalk

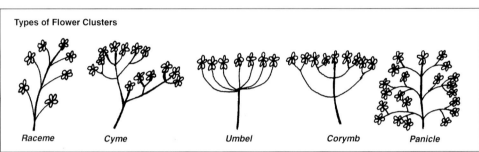

Types of Flower Clusters

Raceme Cyme Umbel Corymb Panicle

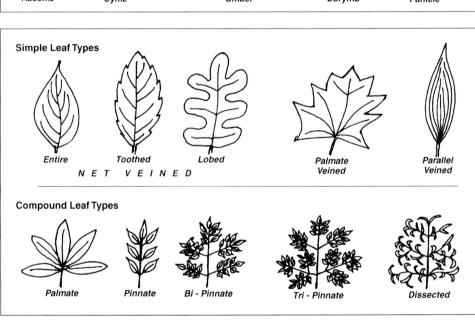

Simple Leaf Types

Entire Toothed Lobed Palmate Veined Parallel Veined

N E T   V E I N E D

Compound Leaf Types

Palmate Pinnate Bi - Pinnate Tri - Pinnate Dissected

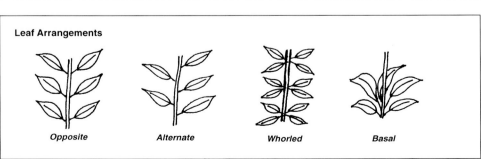

Leaf Arrangements

Opposite Alternate Whorled Basal

O n reflection, there seems to have been no particular time or occasion on which we first said, "We should try to put together a book on wildflowers!" The prospect and concept of doing so only gradually emerged, wishfully and fleetingly at first, but eventually becoming a consciously accepted and realistic goal. Our motivation for doing so also became clearer with the passage of time.

The prime motivation for the book originated from the flowers themselves, particularly from those on the island portion of the Province, where their prevalence, diversity, beauty and intricate detail deserve to be more fully recognized and appreciated as a part of our natural heritage. We have therefore attempted to identify, describe and present to you each of the different wildflowers encountered during our travels around the province. It must be noted however, that our travels have not been all-encompassing. There are extensive areas that we have not yet had the opportunity to explore, each undoubtedly containing many different types of natural habitat. Nor is it likely that we shall ever find ourselves in the position of having seen all there is to see.

As a matter of additional interest we have also included with each flower description a reference to the approximate location and time of year photographed, and provided a map, as an appendix, on which each location is shown with a number coinciding with the photograph number. Where space permits we have also included photographs, scenic and otherwise, relevant to locations or activities mentioned in the text. Occasionally, or perhaps it may be more appropriate to say "throughout", we have also taken the liberty of embellishing some of the texts with:

- *Clarification of botanic terms;*
- *Elaboration on biological processes;*
- *Philosophic or emotionally motivated comment, sometimes in poetic form;*
- *History, geography or economy of some flower locations;*
- *Some salient and not so salient environmental aspects and personal observations.*

It is our hope that these comments, casual asides and observations will relieve what may otherwise be a rather boring repetition of descriptive text, and that you may instead find this book to be interesting, informative and useful in furthering your appreciation of the world of wildflowers so readily and abundantly present here in our province.

The plant kingdom includes algae, mosses, ferns and seed-bearing plants. The seed-bearing plants include the "wildflowers" with which this book is concerned, but also includes trees, woody shrubs, reeds and grasses, which are not intended for coverage here. It is, however, thus made clear that, although wildflowers are a strongly obvious presence in our environment, they represent only a portion of the plant kingdom.

The flowers presented here are divided into two basic groups. The first and largest group is "dicotyledons"– those in which the seedling has two seed-leaves (cotyledons). The second is "monocotyledons"– those characterized by only one leaf on the seedling. These two divisions are further divided into "families", being broad groupings of the scientifically recognized classification system into which flowers exhibiting similar basic characteristics (such as having the same number of petals, sepals, stamens, and ovary cells) are placed. These families are arranged in the usually accepted order of presentation which is intended to reflect the presently perceived order of floral evolution. One must not take from this that evolution has occurred in a linear manner as indicated by the consecutive presentation of families, but must realize that it has actually occurred in a branching manner, commonly typified as a "tree of life", which is incapable of portrayal by means of consecutive listing.

Flowers classified within each family are numbered consecutively and given their common name (or names), followed by their latin or latinized scientific name in italics. The scientific name has two parts:

- *The first is the "genus" name, given to a group of species within a family which exhibit similar characteristics. There may be many "genera" making up a family, and there may be only one species of a genus observed growing in Newfoundland.*

- *The second is the species name, unique to that particular type of flower or plant, and is given as a latinized name relating to some distinguishing feature of the plant or the environment in which it is commonly found, or relating to the name of a person or place.*

A "variety" of a species may occur having minor variations of colour, size, petal arrangement or other characteristic. Occasionally, as a result of further scientific investigation, a variety may be determined to be more appropriately classed as a separate species; or a species determined to be more properly classed in a different genus. In fact, with the passage of time and progress of scientific thought, together with improved scientific techniques for distinguishing differences, much of the naming system (taxonomy) has become rather plastic, depending on reference sources used and whether these sources tend to lump things together or separate minutely. In this regard we have been influenced by a variety of sources as noted in the bibliography and consequently have made some arbitrary decisions in naming and classification. However, we feel that this has been done within a fairly conservative framework.

In several instances we have not been able to identify a flower. Rather than omitting any reference to these we have placed them with the flower genus or species which seems to be most closely related and described them as best we could, leaving it to you or some other reader to assist in their proper identification.

A glossary of botanical terms used in the descriptions is provided at the back of the book in the realization that many of these terms are not in common everyday use and that a convenient reference would be useful. Two indexes are also provided at the back of the book: one for the alphabetic listing of common names of flowers; and the other for the listing of scientific names. In the latter case, genus names are listed alphabetically and species names are listed alphabetically in conjunction with the genus name.

For those interested in photography, all the photographs in this book were taken using a Pentax MG camera, usually fitted with a 55 mm Vivitar 80–200 mm 1:4.0 macro focusing zoom lens, but sometimes using a Pentax-M 1:2 50 mm lens. Photographic films most commonly used were Kodachrome 200 and Ektachrome 200 slide film. In some instances Ektachrome 400 slide film was used and found to be particularly beneficial when using macro lens settings in deep shade while attempting to retain some depth of focus. Occasionally Kodachrome 64 and Ektachrome 100 were used, either because that was the type of film in the camara at the time, (You never know when or where a new flower will rear its head!) or it was the only type available in a remote rural location. In general, the 200 speed film was found to be most adaptable to the variety of light conditions encountered – from fog to bright sun and from exposed locations to deep shade. All of these extremes sometimes being encountered during the same morning or afternoon.

We have derived a great deal of pleasure from our wildflower explorations and, as an added bonus, we now find that we have developed a heightened awareness of our surroundings as we travel through this wonderful province of ours. It is our hope that this book will be helpful to you in increasing your appreciation of the many aspects of natural beauty here in Newfoundland and Labrador.

Contents

Dicotyledons

Contents (continued)

Monocotyledons

FAMILIES

Appendices

1-1   1-1A   2-1

2-2

"The Narrows"
Entry to St. John's Harbour, flanked by Signal Hill and Southside Hills. Harbour frontage in foreground was the site of the first railway termin (1881–1900), later moved to t. west end of the City.

Dicotyledons

1. NETTLE FAMILY
(*Urticaceae*)

Square-stemmed, tallish plants having sharply-toothed, usually paired, simple leaves. Some have stinging hairs on stem and leaves. Flowers are unisexual (sometimes on separate plants), very small, greenish-white, lacking petals, and occur in racemes from leaf axils.

1. STINGING NETTLE
(*Urtica dioica*)

A tall, unbranched plant with paired, short-stalked, coarsely toothed, heart-shaped leaves. Its stem and leaves are densely covered with stinging hairs. Flowers droop or dangle in multiple, slender, sometimes branching racemes from leaf axils. The species name *"dioica"* indicates that it is a "dioecious" plant (male and female flowers occur on separate plants). This appears to be the case in photograph 1-1, taken in late-July in the now-deserted railway yard, Water Street West, St. John's.

1A.

Flowers of the Nettle Family are generally "monoecious" (male and female flowers occur separately, but on the same plant). This example, found on Green Gardens Trail in Gros Morne National Park in late-July, shows characteristics of *U. dioica*, but note green flowers on the upper end of the stem and cream-coloured flowers lower down. Also note leaf-like stipules at the base of leaf stalks; and the stem is not so densely covered with stinging hairs. It may be *U. viridis* (*Green Nettle*) as described by Fernald, but noted as a variety of *U. dioica* by Rouleau.

2. SMARTWEED FAMILY
(*Polygonaceae*)

Plants having numerous, small, inconspicuous flowers often appearing as green, red or brown nutlets or bulbils along the stem and sometimes being white and petal-like. The flower has 3–6 sepals; 4–9 stamens; and a superior ovary. Leaves are alternate, usually untoothed, and the stem is often sheathed at the nodes.

1. BISTORT
(*Polygonum bistorta*)

A dense cylindrical spike of tiny pink flowers atop a smooth, grass-like, unbranched stem up to 3 ft. tall. Note the sheathed enlargement at stem nodes. Upper leaves are long-oval, pointed, untoothed, unstalked and clasp the stem. Lower leaves are more triangular in shape and have a fringed stalk. As flowers mature the stamens extend beyond the petal-like pink sepals, giving the flower spike a fuzzy appearance. The photograph shows part of a large mass growing in early July

beside Topsail Road where it passes through the Town of Paradise. At first glance it looked like a patch of Meadow Foxtail (*Alopecurus pratensis*), a type of grass, but seemed too pink for this and so warranted closer inspection.

2. ALPINE SMARTWEED
(*Polygonum viviparum*)

A small, single-stemmed plant which may be only 2 or 3 inches tall in exposed locations, but may be 6–8 inches in more protected locations. Flowers are in a spike-like

1

raceme, the lower portion of the raceme often being comprised of greenish-brown bulbils rather than flowers. Leaves are narrow-oval, the stem leaves usually sessile and basal leaves stalked. The example shown is a relatively tall specimen found growing in mid-July at Green Point in Gros Morne National Park.

3. LADY'S THUMB/REDLEG
(*Polygonum persicaria*)

An erect or prostrate, branching weed with tight clusters of small greenish-white (sometimes pink) flowers arising from leaf axils. The stem is smooth and reddish with growth nodes encased in a white sheath (ochrea). Leaves are narrow, lanceolate and untoothed. The prostrate example shown was photographed alongside Thorburn Road, St. John's in mid-September. In the lower right-hand corner is a Common Groundsel *(Senecio vulgaris)*.

4. PALE SMARTWEED
(*Polygonum lapathifolium*)

Similar to an erect Lady's Thumb but taller (up to 5 ft.). The stem is green; leaves are larger and broader (hence sometimes called Dock-leaved Smartweed); flower clusters usually greenish-white, longer and tend to arch downwards. The example shown was growing in late-August, in a ditch beside the highway at Topsail Hill, near St. John's.

5. COMMON SMARTWEED/ WATER-PEPPER
(*Polygonum hydropiper*)

Similar to Pale Smartweed except that the flower racemes are longer and the flowers more widely spaced. The example shown was growing in the same roadside ditch at Topsail Hill as the previous example. Also occurring in the ditch at the time, as shown in the photograph, were Willow Herbs *(Epilobium glandulosum)*, Beggar Ticks *(Bidens frondosa)* and Spotted Touch-me-not *(Impatiens capensis)*.

5A.

Perhaps merely a more long-trailing variety of *P. hydropiper*, this purple-stemmed plant with long, trailing racemes and flowers even more widely spaced, was growing on a riverbank at Whitbourne in mid-August. *P. sagittatum* (see below) is seen in the background growing higher up the riverbank.

6. ARROW-LEAVED TEAR THUMB
(*Polygonum sagittatum*)

Rounded, tight terminal clusters of white flowers on 1–4 ft. stems lined with 4 rows of downward-pointing, small prickly barbs extending along the entire length of the stem. Leaves are arrow-shaped and clasp the stem. The example shown was growing on a riverbank at Whitbourne in mid-August (see above).

6A.

A somewhat similar specimen, each stem bearing a globular terminal cluster of green and pink bulbils. Long-stalked, arrow-shaped leaves arise from the base of the stem. Stem leaves are sessile, alternating, arrow-shaped and clasping. The stem and basal leaf stalks are covered with fine white hairs, but there are no barbs. It was found growing in Bowring Park, St. John's in mid-June.

7. ERECT KNOTWEED
(*Polygonum achoreum*)

Pairs of oval, untoothed, short-stalked leaves arise from pale-sheathed growth nodes on an erect, smooth (sometimes ridged) stem. Groups of small white flowers with pale green sepals occur in the leaf axils. A whorl of leaves terminates the stem. The example shown was growing near Confederation Building, St. John's, in late-September.

8. PROSTRATE KNOTWEED
(*Polygonum aviculare*)

A much-branched, prostrate, smooth-stemmed knotweed having clusters of tiny flowers in the axils of alternating, small,

2-3

2-8

2-4

2-5

2-5A

2-6

2-6A

2-7

2-9

2-10

2-11

2-12

2-13

"Railway Station"
Designed by W.H. Massey of the Reid Newfoundland Railway Company and built in 1902. It is now the St. John's terminal for the Canadian National Roadcruiser Bus Service across the Island.

oval, sessile or short-stalked leaves. The example shown was growing in late-August on a beach in Trinity Bay, near Backside Pond Camping Park. We camped at this park on many occasions while the children were young and have returned occasionally in more recent years. There is a pleasant walking trail leading from the Park to a nearby coastal beach, thence along the beach and through a wood to a grassy embankment overlooking the bay.

9. BLACK BINDWEED
(*Polygonum convolvulus*)
A climbing or prostrate plant with thin, reddish stems. Leaves are triangular to hastate, stalked, untoothed with edges tending to roll under, and are evenly spaced along the stem. Flowers occur in short-stalked clusters arising from leaf axils. The example shown was growing on the gravel shoulder of the highway, near the entrance to Donovans Industrial Park, Mount Pearl, in early-October.

10. JAPANESE KNOTWEED
(*Polygonum cuspidata/ Reynoutria japonica*)
A tall bamboo-like plant growing to a height of 6 ft. or more, often forming a thicket due to the invasiveness of its creeping rhizomes. The stem is smooth, hollow, sometimes angular, and may be an inch or more across. Branches and leaves arise from growth nodes. Leaves are large and triangular. Many-branched flower spikes of small white flowers arise from the growth nodes. These flower spikes may vary from small 6-inch clusters to extensive flower plumes 3 ft. or more in length. The example shown is from a small forest of them in our back yard. We have been at pains to discourage these since they first appeared from a truckload of fill more than 20 years ago. However, we believe we have finally reached an understanding with it because it no longer seems determined to occupy more space and we have not

seriously attacked it during the past few years. It dies back each fall necessitating the removal of dried canes. In younger years we commonly used sections of these stems as pea-blowers, then readily available from a forest of them growing along the Empire Avenue embankment just north of Circular Road. Empire Avenue was a railway track route during the early days of railroading when the railway terminal was near the present location of Hotel Newfoundland.

11. SHEEP SORREL
(*Rumex acetosella*)
A low-growing, multi-stemmed plant bearing long, ascending, loosely spaced spikes of small reddish or greenish flowers. Male (staminate) and female (pistillate) flowers grow on separate plants. Leaves are spear-shaped and occur mainly near the base of the stem. Smaller and narrower leaves also occur at the growth nodes from which the flower spikes arise. The example shown was growing in early-July at Marystown on a knoll overlooking the shipyard.

12. GARDEN SORREL
(*Rumex acetosa*)
Similar to *R. acetosella*, but taller (up to 3 ft.) with flower spikes not so strongly ascending, giving it a feathery or plume-like appearance. The example shown was growing in late June in the flood-plain of a stream through Bowring Park.

13. CURLED DOCK
(*Rumex crispus*)
Short spikes of closely whorled green flowers rise sharply from leaf axils on the upper portion of a single stout stem. Its long leaves have strongly waved edges.("Curled", "undulate", "crisped" are other terms commonly used to describe this leaf-edge condition.) Lower leaves are triangular, dry up and fall off in mid-season. Upper leaves are long and lanceolate. The example shown is of a young plant growing in June near the CBC building

on Prince Philip Parkway, St. John's. Note the large thick lower leaves and the emerging flower spikes.

13A.
A more mature plant growing in July near the western end of Long Pond on MUN Campus. To the right, a tall mustard is going to seed (probably *Barbarea vulgaris*). Gray's Manuel of Botany (Fernald) notes that a hybrid of *R. crispus* with *R. obtusifolius* occurs in Newfoundland and other eastern provinces. As a result, these species may be found to be quite variable.

14. BROAD-LEAVED DOCK
(*Rumex obtusifolius*)
Similar to *R. crispus* but flower spikes not so tightly ascendant and flower whorls more widely separated. Broad lower leaves are long-stalked, heart-shaped at the base and usually red-veined with a distinctively arched venation. Leaf margins are only slightly wavy. The example shown was growing in late-July in a vacant lot on Water Street West.

15. MEXICAN DOCK
(*Rumex mexicanus*)
A tall, stout-stemmed, water loving species with large, upright, dense, nearly leafless flower spikes. Lower leaves are lanceolate, quite long (18 inches or more), acute at both ends, and have slightly wavy margins. The example shown was photographed in September at Power's Pond, off Thorburn Road near the recently revised western boundary of the City of St. John's.

The Sentinel

Stealthily the enemy
occupies the land;
Surrounding, infiltrating,
urged on at our command.
Mindless enemies of earth
about us everywhere;
Riding river currents,
sailing the evening air.

Who keeps watch at the riverbank?
Who scans the evening sky?
Who will issue a challenge clear
when the enemy is nigh?
Slowly, silently, certainly
a doomsday plan is laid.
Who harkens to the sentinel
when a call to arms is made?

What do we know of the enemy's
insideous arms array?
What strategy has been devised
to keep the enemy at bay?
What is our first line of defense?
What level of loss will we take?
Do we still think the earth exists
only for our sake?

Slowly, oh so slowly
the enemy proceeds.
Generations come and go
as flower and as seeds.
There on the riverbank
a sentinel stands tall.
How many will be martyred
before we heed the call?

3. GOOSEFOOT FAMILY
(*Chenopodiaceae*)
The family is comprised mainly of weedy herbs and includes a number of common vegetables, such as beet and spinach, not relevant to this presentation. Flowers are small and usually green, in tight clusters or racemes rising from leaf axils. They do not have petals but are composed of 3–5 sepals fused around the sexual parts. Male and female flowers (staminate and pistillate) may be separate on the same plant (monoecious) or combined (hermaphrodite). Leaves are quite variable but commonly spear-shaped (hastate) or like the imprint of a web-footed bird – hence "goosefoot".

Burton's Pond:
Once a favourite skating area on the outskirts
of St. John's, is now a small park-like area
and waterfowl refuge within memorial
University Campus. Student residences are
seen in the background.

2-13A

2-14

Mill Pond:
Industrial
water supply
for the Corner
Brook paper
mill, this
pond is
located in
front of
Glynmill Inn.
Beyond is Sir
Richard
Squires
Building,
housing
government
offices.

2-15

3-1   3-1A   3-2

3-3   3-4

Glynmill Inn:
A tudor style hotel in the heart of Corner Brook, still reflects the ambience of the 20's and 30's when the paper company town was established.

1. LAMB'S QUARTERS
(*Chenopodium album*)
A variable, erect, branching plant. Flowers are tiny, greenish and may be in the form of interrupted spikes, panicles or cymes arising from leaf axils. Large lower leaves may be whitish beneath and narrowly to broadly rhombic or ovate with broadly toothed or wavy edges. Upper stem leaves may be untoothed and lanceolate or even linear. The stem may be ridged, reddish tinged, and red-streaked at branch junctures. The flowers of the genus *Chenopodium* are hermaphroditic, distinguishing them from those of the genus *Atriplex* which are monoecious. This specimen shows the typical interrupted spikes of tiny green flowers rising from axils of narrowly lanceolate, untoothed leaves of the upper stem. It was growing in late-August at Mary's Harbour on the southern coast of Labrador.

1A.
This example of the variability of Lamb's Quarters shows the sturdy, erect stem and its usually branching character. Larger rhombic, deltoid and lanceolate leaves are confined to the lower stem. The upper stem is almost devoid of leaves. Flowers are in thick hanging panicles. A smaller specimen to the left of the picture exhibits more of the narrow lanceolate leaves on the upper stem and its flowers are spike-like rather than panicled. These were growing in late-August among Canada Thistle (*Cirsium arvense*) just west of the CBC Building on Prince Philip Drive.

2. OAK-LEAVED GOOSEFOOT
(*Chenopodium glaucum*)
Flower spikes are fewer and clusters (glomerules) more widely spaced than in Lamb's Quarters. Leaves have wavy edges (similar to oak leaves); are sessile or very short stalked; and do not vary significantly in size or shape throughout the plant. Usually a prostrate plant, the example shown is erect, but the stem curvature indi-

cates its innate weakness. It was growing in early-October at Corner Brook near Glynmill Inn.

The City of Corner Brook, on the south side of Bay of Islands at the mouth of the Humber River, was an area sparsely settled by fishermen-farmers during the 18th and 19th centuries. A pulp and paper mill, constructed there in 1925, resulted in rapid urbanization centred on a planned company town known as "Townsite". Peripheral community growth became known as Humbermouth, Corner Brook East, Corner Brook West, and Curling. These were separately incorporated towns during the 1940's and were amalgamated in 1955 into a City of 25,000 people. Glynmill Inn, central to the initial Townsite, has been substantially modernized, but still reflects the ambience of the '20's and '30's.

3. PIGWEED
(*Chenopodium lanceolatum*)
An erect plant with strongly ascending branches. Leaves are long-ovate or lanceolate with few rounded teeth or lobes. Long leaf-stalks are a notable characteristic. Flowers are in slender, interrupted, upright spikes or cymes. Note also that minor occurrences of rhombic and other leaf forms are present on the same plant. The example shown was also growing in early-October near Glynmill Inn, Corner Brook.

4. COMMON ORACHE
(*Atriplex patula*)
A simple or branching, slender-stemmed plant commonly found in saline or alkaline soil. Flowers occur in spikes from leaf axils of the upper leaves. Male and female flowers are separate on the same plant (monoecious). Leaves may be triangular, arrow-shaped or ovate and sometimes with basal lobes (hastate), very similar to Lamb's Quarters (*C. album*). The example shown was growing in a highway ditch on Topsail Hill in early September.

5

4. PINK FAMILY
(*Caryophyllaceae*)

This family is comprised of small herbs having radially symmetrical flowers, usually 5-petalled with petals variously cleft into 2-lobes. However, petals may be absent and with sepals only. The number of stamens are usually twice the number of sepals; and there may be 2 to 5 styles.

1. LESSER STITCHWORT
(*Stellaria graminea*)

Long, slender, branching stem with relatively few, paired narrow leaves. Flowers have 5 white petals and 5 green, sharply pointed sepals about half the petal length. The petals are deeply, almost fully divided, so that the flower appears to have 10 petals. The example shown was growing in the latter part of August, about half way up Mt. Scio, St. John's, within a cleared powerline reservation.

2. COMMON CHICKWEED
(*Stellaria media*)

Flowers have 5 white, deeply divided petals similar to *S. graminea*. Sepals are broad and longer than petals. Stamens are much shorter than in *S. graminea*. Leaves are paired, pointed oval, upper ones have no leaf stalk. The example shown was growing at Charlottetown, Labrador in early September.

3. MOUSE-EAR CHICKWEED
(*Cerastium vulgatum*)

Petals are notched rather than deeply divided and sepals are about the same length as petals. The stem and paired, oval, stalkless leaves are covered with a fuzz of short, white hair. The example shown was photographed in my backyard in mid-June.

4. ALPINE CHICKWEED
(*Cerastium alpinum*)

Similar in its hairiness to *C. vulgatum,* but of a more clumping nature made more pronounced by the occurance of numerous leaves along the lower stem. The weak upper stem bears only 1 or 2 small, linear, clasping, bract-like leaves. Stems bear comparatively few terminal flowers. Sepals are much shorter than petals. The example shown was growing at Cape Norman in mid-July.

Cape Norman is one of the most northerly points of the Great Northern Peninsula and is characterized by extensive tracts of exposed calcareous conglomerate rock.

5. BERING SEA CHICKWEED
(*Cerastium beeringianum*)

A low-growing form of *Cerastium* having small ovate basal leaves forming a mat around the flower clump. Less conspicuously hairy than *C. alpinum*; basal leaves not as dense; and sepals only slightly shorter than petals. These were growing at Watt's Point Calcareous Barrens in mid-July.

6. MOUNTAIN SANDWORT
(*Arenaria groenlandica*)

A low-growing, matted plant having whorls of bright green, needle-like leaves on the lower stem and pairs of small reddish bract-like leaves on the upper stem. The flower has 5 white, spatulate petals. Sepals are shorter than petals. The example shown has only one flower per stem and was growing in mid-July at the base of Table Mountain, on the road to Trout River in Gros Morne National Park.

Table Mountain is the spectacular result of cataclysmic movement of the earth's tectonic plates in geologically recent (palaeozoic) times. Since first visiting the area on completion of the highway across the Island in 1965, we have always referred to it as "the mountains of the moon" because of its singularly barren, yellow-brown, boulder-strewn appearance. Extensive patches of snow remain on the side of the mountain

6

4-1

Cape Norman:
Located at the northern extremity of The Great Northern Peninsula, it is characterized by extensive tracts of calcareous conglomerate rock.

4-2

4-4

4-3

4-6

4-5

4-7

4-8

4-9

4-10

4-11

4-12

throughout the year, providing opportunity for fun, frolic and cool relief to those who undertake the fairly arduous climb to the top in summertime.

7. GROVE SANDWORT
(*Arenaria lateriflora*)
A sandwort with grey, twiggy stems and elliptical, paired leaves, commonly found in moist soil conditions. The example shown was growing in early July at Indian Head Park, Stephenville.

8. BEACH SANDWORT
(*Arenaria peploides*)
A member of the sandwort genus adapted to wet, even inundated, conditions along stream beds, beaches and riverbanks. The flower when fully open has flat, white, paddle-shaped petals; 5 stamens and a single, rotund pistil; pointed, broad sepals as long as, or longer, than petals. (Its reproductive composition is somewhat different from the typical *Arenaria*, and it is commonly classed in a separate genus as *Honkenya peploides*.) The plant is succulent overall, with cream-coloured stems arising from similar and usually extensive runners. Paired, pointed-ovate, closely spaced leaves clasp the stem, each pair at right-angles to successive pairs.

The example shown was photographed in mid-July alongside a tidal pool at Gooseberry Cove Picnic Park on the east side of Placentia Bay, south of Placentia. In other instances where we have seen these, such as at Cow Head in Gros Morne National Park, the petals were noticeably smaller and the stamens were arched inwards over the pistil.

9. ALPINE CAMPION
(*Lychnis alpina*)
A cluster of 5-petalled, rose-purple flowers atop an 8-inch stem, usually with secondary flower stalks arising from the upper leaf axils. The smooth, dark purple stem has paired, lance-shaped, clasping leaves ascend-ing at an acute angle. The example shown was growing on the slope of Table Mountain, Gros Morne National Park in late July.

10. RED CAMPION
(*Lychnis dioica*)
Stalked clusters of red to pink 5-petalled flowers atop branching stems up to 2 ft. or more high. Petals are 2-lobed, spread flatly around the opening to a long and inflated calyx tube, and are sometimes overlapping. A ring of white stamens surrounds the tube opening. Wine-red sepals are fused forming a calyx tube and are covered with whitish hairs. Flower stalks are also hairy. Leaves are paired, pointed-elliptical and, in the photograph, are turning brown with maturity. The example shown was growing in mid-August near Tors Cove on the Southern Shore Road. This road (highway) runs south from St. John's along the east coast of the Avalon Peninsula and is quite scenic. It also includes points of historic significance, such as the community of Calvert, the site of William Vaughan's attempt at colonization in 1616 and later efforts by Sir George Calvert (Lord Baltimore) commencing in 1621.

11. MOSS CAMPION
(*Silene acaulis*)
Many tiny pink flowers covering a cushion of small, densely crowded leaves. The petals are oval and have a small notch. The photograph was taken in mid-July near the bird sanctuary at Cape St. Mary's. We have also found these growing in quite large tussocks at Watt's Point Calcareous Barrens at about the same time of year.

12. SEA-SPURRY
(*Spergularia marina*)
A small, pink 5-petalled flower arising from long, sometimes prostrate stems capable of rooting at nodes, and hence may be considered as runners. Sepals are as long as, or longer, than petals. Narrow, linear leaves are in whorls, sometimes one-sided whorls, at the nodes. Small, paired, leaf-like

appendages (stipules) occur where the stem branches. The picture was taken near the Health Sciences Centre, St. John's in early September. The large, hairy leaves in the background are probably those of Black Knapweed (*Centaurea nigra*).

5. BUTTERCUP/CROWFOOT FAMILY
(*Ranunculaceae*)

Petals, when present, are the same number as sepals, usually 5, but may vary from 3 to 15. Where petals are absent, sepals may be coloured and look like petals. Both stamens and pistils may be numerous and clustered in the centre of the flower.

1. WHITE WATER-CROWFOOT
(Ranunculus aquatilis)

Usually found as a tangle of long, whitish stems floating just below the surface of still water. These stems bear two types of leaves: finely disected ones which act like roots, and palmate ones floating at or just below the water surface. Only the small white 5-petalled, yellow-centred flowers project above the water. A mass of these were floating in a protected lagoon formed by the wharf and boathouse at the Whitbourne Community Park in mid-July.

2. SPEARWORT
(*Ranunculus flammula*)

Little 5-petalled yellow flowers on thin stalks with narrow leaves, growing from rooting nodes of surface runners in moist locations such as sandy shorelines. Those shown were growing on the shoreline of Jack's Pond in mid-August.

3. COMMON BUTTERCUP
(*Ranunculus acris*)

Flowers have 5 broad shiny-yellow petals surrounding an inner circle of stamens and pistils. Petals are underlaid by 5 pointed green sepals about half the length of the petals. Flowers occur at the extremity of erect branching stems up to 3 feet high. Stem leaves occur as linear to narrow-lobed whorls at stem joints. Basal leaves are long-stalked and terminate in 5 deeply lobed, palmate segments. The example shown was growing

at the base of the White Hills, near Quidi Vidi Lake, St. John's, in late-June. By way of seasonal comparision we have also found this buttercup growing at Charlottetown, a small community on the coast of Labrador, north of Port Hope Simpson, in early-September

Quidi Vidi Lake is the focus for a good deal of outdoor recreational activity in St. John's; from rowing, laser-sailing and wind-surfing on the pond, to walking and jogging around its perimeter. The Lake is also the venue for the Royal St. John's Regatta, a day of fixed-seat rowing competition using 6-oared racing shells. Teams begin practice as soon as "ice is off the pond". A local holiday for the event is held on the first Wednesday in August or first suitable day thereafter. The first record-ed Regatta held on Quidi Vidi Lake was in 1826, but such competitions were held pre-viousely on St. John's Harbour.

4. CREEPING BUTTERCUP
(*Ranunculus repens*)

Grows by surface runners from which new leaves arise and new roots and stems may emerge if a suitable rooting medium is found. The example shown has more than the usual number of petals and the leaves do not clearly display the white blotches or markings typical of the species. It was grow-ing near the front corner of our house in early-June.

5-1

5-2

5-3

Annual Regatta: *(Above)*
Fixed-seat racing shells ready to start the
"Championship Race" at the 169th Regatta,
Quidi Vidi Lake, St. John's.

Cape Race Lighthouse: *(Right)*
Located at the southeast tip of the Avalon Peninsula,
this beacon had been tended by the Myrick Family
since 1874, but became automated in 1994.

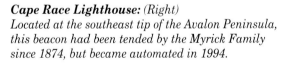

5-4

5-5

5-6B

5-6

5-6A

5-7

5-8

5. TALL MEADOW-RUE
(*Thalictrum polygamum*)

A tall, bushy, wetlands plant growing to 6 feet or more. On close inspection the fuzzy white flowers reveal themselves to be small "star bursts" of numerous stamens. The flower has no petals, and the pale green sepals which initially encase the flower bud, soon become gauze-like and fall away. The plant's compound leaves are comprised of paired, oval to elliptical leaflets, the tip of the terminal leaflet being 3-toothed. The example shown was growing in mid-July beside the highway at Cormack, a farming community near Deer Lake. The yellow flowers in the background are Golden Ragwort (*Senecio aureus*).

6. SMALL-FLOWERED ANEMONE
(*Anemone parviflora*)

Has 5 white, petal-like sepals, (rarely 6 or 7) tinged purplish-blue on the under-surface, surrounding a central cluster of numerous yellow stamens and styles. Shiny, 3-part, wedge-shaped basal leaves are toothed on the outer edge. A whorl of similar leaves occurs about half-way up the otherwise leafless stem. These low-growing flowers (up to 6-inches high) were growing quite profusely in mid-July along the edge of the old roadway following the shoreline through Watt's Point Calcareous Barrens.

6A.

This little flower, about 4-inches high, was growing at Watt's Point Calcareous Barrens in mid-June (a month earlier than the foregoing, but in a different year). It has features similar to *A. parviflora*, but leaflets of the basal leaf are rounder; there is no apparent whorl of leaves at mid-stem; the flower appears to be comprised of 3 white petals, 3 smaller white sepals and a central cluster with short stamen filaments. It is inserted here in an undefined status merely as an item of interest.

6B.

This seems to be a reasonable place to insert this indeterminate little flower which was growing in a sphagnum bog near a newly developing summer cabin area in the Deer Park off Salmonier Line. It was flowering at the same time as the bake-apple (*R. chamaemorus*) and has 11 long white sepals or petals. Unfortunately the finer features of the flower's centre are not clearly portrayed, but it bears a striking resemblence to Wood Anemone (*A. nemorosa*).

7. MARSH MARIGOLD/COWSLIP
(*Caltha palustris*)

A large, buttercup-type flower with 5 or 6 bright yellow sepals. It has both basal leaves and stem leaves, all of which are round or kidney-shaped. Usually found growing along river banks. Those shown were growing alongside a small stream in Gros Morne National Park in early-June.

8. GOLDTHREAD
(*Coptis groenlandica*)

A small woodland flower growing from light-toned runners, from which the common name is derived. The flower has 5–7 petal-like sepals; the same number of tiny yellow-cupped petals (staminoids); numerous white-tipped stamens; and a slender style in the centre (seen more clearly in the photograph by its shadow on the upper sepal). Its 3-part basal leaves are not clearly discernable from the photograph. Note the tiny, pointed leaf projecting from a node or joint about two-thirds up the bare and slender stem. This specimen was photographed at Watt's Point Calcareous Barrens in mid-July. Others of the same species growing at Aspen Brook near Grand Falls, had achieved the same state of growth in mid-June of the same year.

9. COMMON MONKSHOOD
(Aconitum napellus)

Although the leaves are very similar to the Buttercup, the flowers are quite irregular. Its five petal-like sepals are white with a bluish-purple tinge throughout, the tinge being most prominent along the leading edges. The flower is bilaterally symmetrical, the upper sepal being enlarged, deeply cupped and protrudes forward forming a hood in which the nectaries are hidden, these nectaries being the only remnants of petals. These were photographed in Forteau, on the Labrador side of the Strait of Belle Isle, in mid-September. They are undoubtedly garden escapes, but seem to escape rather easily, having been observed in substantial colonies continuing to flourish in and around vacated and long-forgotten gardens as may be found in many locations throughout the province.

10. COLUMBINE
(Aquilegia vulgaris)

Commonly found as garden escapes in moist to dry soil. Pink to pale-purple flowers droop from the top of sparsely-leaved, purplish stems growing to 3 ft. in height. Its five petals and five sepals are the same colour, but petals have long hollow spurs containing the nectaries and extend back from the base of the flower. Sepals have short spurs without nectaries. Leaves are usually in threes with 3 leaflets per leaf-stalk, the terminal leaflet being 3-lobed. The example shown was growing in marshy ground off Higgins Line near Confederation Building, St. John's in late-June.

6. WATER-LILY FAMILY
(Nymphaceae)

Aquatic plants growing in muddy-bottomed, still-water ponds, each plant producing a single flower and several to many leaves. Flowers and leaves are on separate, often quite long, stalks sufficient for the flower and leaf to reach the surface of the water.

1. BULL-HEAD/YELLOW POND LILY
(Nuphar veriegatum)

The flower is composed of an outer ring of 5–6 stiff, yellow, petal-like sepals which cup the similer but smaller yellow petals. At the centre is a disc-shaped stigma surrounded by a cluster of stamens. Leaves are floating and broadly oval with a narrow notch and rounded basal lobes at the leaf stalk. Flower stalks rise 2–4 inches above the water surface. Leaf stalks are curved near the surface enabling them to accommodate to changing water levels. The example shown was growing in early-August in a sheltered cove of Southwest Pond, near the junction of the Trans-Canada Highway and Salmonier Line. A similar but small-flowered and small-leafed species *(Nuphar microphyllum)*, also occurs in Newfoundland, and is recognizable by its red rather than yellow disc-shaped stigma.

2. FRAGRANT WATER-LILY
(Nymphaea odorata)

Numerous white petals in concentric rings surrounding similarly numerous yellow stamens. The flowers open in sunlight when released by the otherwise constraining influence of 4 brownish-green sepals. Leaves are round and floating and have a narrow notch extending to the slightly off-centre juncture with the leaf-stalk. The example shown was growing in early-August in a small pond surrounded by a sphagnum bog beside the roadway near Smith Sound. Brown markings on the leaves were made by a red water-beetle, seen on the leaf between the two flowers.

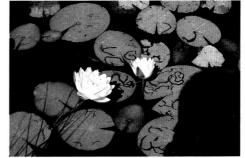

Strait of Belle Isle Ferry:
Docking at Blanc Sablon on the Quebec-Labrador Boundary, after an approximately two-hour trip from St. Barbe on the Island's Great Northern Peninsula.

5-9

Confederation Building, St. John's:
Looking northward across Prince Philip Drive, Rennie's River in foreground.

5-10

6-1

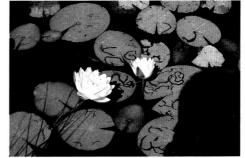

6-2

7-1   8-1   8-2

Nain:
The coastal vessel "Northern Ranger" moored at the public wharf in Nain, the most northerly scheduled port of call on the Labrador Coast.

Marystown:
The ferry "Flanders" nearing completion at the Marystown Shipyard, destined for service between Bell Island and Portugal Cove in Conception Bay.

7. POPPY FAMILY
(*Papaveraceae*)
Large-petalled, usually solitary flowers with 4–6 or 8–12 petals, 2–3 sepals which fall off soon after the bud opens, numerous stamens and a superior ovary. Stems bleed a yellow, red or white sap when broken. Leaves are usually deeply lobed and basal.

1. ICELAND POPPY
(*Papaver nudicaule*)
Large, scarlet (sometimes yellow or white) petals surrounding numerous yellow stamens and a slightly projecting style. A slender hairy stem up to one foot high, drooping when in bud. Sepals enclosing buds are similarly hairy. Numerous lobed, spreading leaves surround the base of the stem. The example shows one group of many such flowers grow-

ing in early-September throughout Nain, an Inuit community of 1000 population. Nain is the most northern permanent community on the coast of Labrador and is the final scheduled port of call of vessels in the marine coastal service before turning southward again. These flowers are escapes from earlier cultivation, but have become quite widespread and naturalized, presenting an attractive, colourful, summerish appearance.

8. MUSTARD FAMILY
(*Cruciferae*)
Flowers 4-petaled, forming a cross (hence the name), and having 6 stamens (4 long and 2 short).

1. SHEPHERD'S PURSE
(*Capsella bursa – pastoris*)
Small, white, 4-petal flowers atop a somewhat hairy stalk rising from a basal rosette of dandelion-like leaves. Few, coarsely toothed, arrow-shaped, hairy leaves clasp the stalk. Seed pods are triangular or heart-shaped. This specimen was found growing near the shoreline at Marystown in early-July. Rouleau notes that "Pick-pocket" is a local name sometimes used for this flower.

Marystown has a population of 7,000 and is the regional centre for the 30,000 or so people concentrated around "the boot" of the Burin Peninsula. Its main industries are shipbuilding and fish processing. Mortier Bay, a large, deep and well-protected bay alongside the town, has for many years been considered a prospective centre for the transshipment of goods between Europe and North America, but nothing of substance along these lines has yet materialized. In recent years the bay has been a refuge for

deep-sea drilling rigs during periods of peak ice conditions and for regular repair and maintenance.

2. NORTHERN WHITLOW-GRASS
(*Draba longipes*)
Tightly bunched, 4-petalled, white flowers atop smooth 6–10 inch stems rising from a small basal rosette of spatulate leaves. Widely separated, elliptical, slightly toothed leaves, smaller than basal leaves, alternate up the stem. The picture was taken in mid-June at the foot of a cliff rising from the beach along the south shore of Rocky Harbour.

We were returning from a trip to Red Bay, on the Labrador side of the Straits of Belle Isle, where we were quite impressed by the archaeological work being done to restore a 16th century Basque whaling factory. A great deal of additional significant work has been done there since then and the area is now designated "A World Heritage Site".

3. ROCK WHITLOW-GRASS
(*Draba norvegica*)

Flowerhead similar to *D. longipes*, but stem shorter (4–5 inches), sturdier and hairy. Broad leaves are lanceolate with a rounded tip and also occur clasping the stem at branch junctions. Fleshy, shiny-green, ovate pods project from the upper stem. The photograph was taken at Watt's Point Calcareous Barrens in mid-July.

3A.

A low, tufted species of *Draba* having stemless white flowers clasped within a rosette of hairy, elliptical, leathery, dark green leaves. It is probably Snow Whitlowgrass (*D. nivalis*), noted by A. E. Porsild in his "Illustrated Flora of the Canadian Archipelago". The example shown was growing at Watt's Point Calcareous Barrens in mid-July. Note also the plant just below it with a radiating rosette of long fleshy leaves. This appears to be one of the Plantain Family, probably Shoreweed (*Littorella uniflora*).

4. DAMES ROCKET
(*Hesperis matronalis*)

Clusters of 4-petalled white, pink or purple flowers bunched atop leafy stems up to 3 ft. tall. Leaves alternate along the stem; have short leaf-stalks; are broad at the base but graduate to a sharp point at the tip, and are slightly toothed along the edges. This flower is a common garden escape, and, in an urban context, has a habit of escaping from garden to garden. The ones shown were growing in our backyard in mid-June, although they were not planted there by human hand.

5. WATERCRESS
(*Nasturtium officinale*)

Panicles of 4-petalled white flowers atop firm, succulent stalks; outer flowers blooming before inner ones. Leaves pinnate with paired, oval, untoothed leaflets; the end leaflet being somewhat larger, rounder and with minor lobes along the margin. The specimen shown was growing on the bank of Virginia River, St. John's in mid-July.

6. COW CRESS/FIELD PENNYCRESS
(*Lepedium campestre*)

A cylindrical raceme of small, white flowers atop multiple stems curving upwards from a clump of untoothed, spatulate basal leaves. A whorl of secondary stems each with a terminal raceme, occurs just below the main raceme. Numerous lance-shaped, toothed leaves clasp the smooth stem. The example shown was growing just west of Long Pond, St. John's in mid-June.

7. SEA-ROCKET
(*Cakile edentula*)

Bunches of 4-petalled, white flowers emerging from a rosette of fleshy, spatulate, blunt-toothed leaves. Stems are smooth, succulent and branched; branches arising from leaf axils. Flower buds may be pale to deep pink prior to opening. The example shown was growing in late-July on the beach at Gooseberry Cove Park where we stopped to eat on a return trip from visiting the sea-bird sanctuary at Cape St. Mary's.

During the nesting period the top of this sea stack, the focal point of the sanctuary, is covered by nesting pairs of gannets. All nooks and crannies of the stack and nearby cliffs are occupied by gannets, murres and kittiwakes. The 250 ft. deep chasm between the stack and the top of the cliff where the viewer may stand, is only a few yards wide, so the nesting birds can be viewed quite closely without disturbance.

7A.

This second picture, taken in late-August at the beach in Backside Pond Park, Trinity Bay, shows the quite different form of a mature Sea-rocket. Note the long recumbent racemes of pods, still with a few flowers showing; the longer strap-like leaves; and the generally prostrate nature of the mature plant.

8-3

8-3A

8-4

8-5

8-6

8-7

8-7A

Cape St. Mary's:
Gannets nesting atop a 250 ft. "sea stack" at Cape St. Mary's Bird Sanctuary may be viewed quite closely without disturbing them.

8-8

8-9

8-10

8-11

8-12

8-13

8. SCURVY-GRASS
(*Cochlearia groenlandica*)

Another seaside member of the mustard family, this species has shorter but broader white petals; smaller ovate to triangular, slightly lobed leaves; spherical pods; sometimes recumbent. This one was growing at The Arches Scenic Site, north of Gros Morne National Park in mid-July.

9. ALPINE ROCK CRESS
(*Arabis alpina*)

Racemes of white flowers atop dark, wood-like stems (caudex). A basal mat of ovate, sharply toothed leaves, with a few clasping, alternating stem leaves. The picture was taken at Watt's Point Calcareous Barrens in mid-June. Note the stony terrain from which a variety of growth is beginning to emerge.

10. HARE'S-EAR MUSTARD
(*Conringia orientalis*)

A rosette of small yellow mustard flowers atop a straight, usually single stalk. Elliptical, untoothed leaves clasp the stem and rise acutely along it. The examples shown were growing in a large vacant area in St. John's where Virginia River crosses Logy Bay Road. The area had been left fallow for quite a few years after completion of residential development in the vicinity. Weeds were thus left to mature and proliferate resulting in quite a thick ever-changing floral groundcover, which some would construe to be an unmitigated mess, while others would see it as a site of natural interest and beauty reflecting seasonal progression. Note the mustard leaves turning red as it matures and the surrounding mayweed on the verge of flowering, while the formative leaves of later wildflowers are just beginning to emerge from the ground.

11. WINTER CRESS/YELLOW ROCKET
(*Barbarea vulgaris*)

Racemes of bright yellow flowers atop numerous, ridged stems up to 2 ft. in height arising from the perennial root. Basal leaves are strongly lobed. Upper leaves are small, triangular, coarsely toothed and clasp the stem. The picture was taken on Memorial University Campus near Burton's Pond in early-June. Burton's Pond was a popular skating site prior to its inclusion into the university campus. It is now a winter wildfowl refuge in conjunction with Rennie's River, Long Pond and Leary's Brook.

12. INDIAN / CHINESE MUSTARD
(*Brassica juncea*)

Pale yellow, 4-petalled flowers, with petals having a distinctive paddle shape. Stem may be smooth or finely speckled with a few short hairs. Stem leaves are broad-oval, coarsely toothed, and variously lobed at the base. The example shown was growing in the narrow strip of soil intended for grass between the curb and sidewalk on University Avenue, St. John's.

13. RAPE/FIELD MUSTARD
(*Brassica napus*)

Taller than most other mustards (up to 3 ft. high), it has large pale-yellow flowers in terminal spikes. Its thick, fleshy, purple-shaded branching stem and clasping lance-shaped leaves are covered with a white fuzz. The example shown was growing in wet meadowland near the Town of Port au Port in mid-July.

This St. George's Bay Area, on the West Coast of the Island, south of Corner Brook, was the site of settlement for many fishermen from the south of France and northern Spain (Basques from the Bay of Biscay) in the 16th century.

Language and customs remained relatively untouched by external influences until the early 1940's when construction of Harmon Air Force Base began as part of Britain's "Lend-Lease" arrangement with the United States during World War II.

14. LADY'S SMOCK/ CUCKOO FLOWER
(*Cardamine pratensis*)

The little vale is green again.
The winter snow is gone.
The path beside the little brook
beckons the walker on
To see the coiling fern unfold
bathing in golden sun;
To feel the cool, fresh softness of
the mossy rock beyond.
Tread once again the stepping stones where
childhood feet had trod;
To stand among the lady's smock
and be a child of God.
Recall the feel of a mother's touch
while toddling by her side;
And once again walk hand in hand
with the girl to be my bride.
Fond memories flood back again
of a beautiful bygone day
When our children were but children
on that path along the way.

First seen in springtime as a white haze over marshy meadows and along river banks, eventually covering the area with a white floral sheet. Buds are pink, but petals are white when open. Basal and stem leaves are compound with many paired leaflets. The flower shown was growing at the western end of Long Pond in late-May 1988, but did not reach this stage of bloom in 1991 until late-June. This is a substantial seasonal variation, attributable in large measure to the vagueries of duration of ice floes carried southward each year by the Labrador Current.

15. BITTERCRESS
(*Cardamine pensylvanica*)
A much smaller plant (3–5 inches) than Lady's Smock, but has similar leaves, correspondingly smaller flowers and a slightly hairy stem. The example shown was growing in our backyard in late-June in a year when spring flowering had been set back by two weeks to a month due to an extended period of unusually low temperatures.

9. SUNDEW FAMILY
(*Droseraceae*)
Small, insectivorous plants of bogs and marshes. White 5-part flowers occur in a terminal cluster atop deep-red leafless stems up to 6–8 inches tall, arising from the centre of a radially spreading basal rosette of leaves. These basal leaves are long-stalked, deep-red to greenish-yellow with round elongated end-lobes ringed with glandular hairs. These hairs attract and enfold insects which are then absorbed by the plant through the action of leaf enzymes. Species in Newfoundland differ only in leaf-shape and as to branching or unbranched flower stem. The example shown is Round-leaved Sundew (*Drosera rotundifolia*) growing in mid-August in shallow water of a sphagnum bog at Seal Cove, Conception Bay.

10. STONECROP FAMILY
(*Crasulaceae*)
Most members of this family are fleshy plants adapted to growing in arid climates. Flowers are usually small and star-shaped in dense terminal clusters or cymes and have 4 or 5 sepals and petals with 1 or 2 stamens per petal. Leaves may be oval or narrow and are generally sessile (unstalked) and alternate along numerous stems radiating from a central root-system. Some species have prostrate stems and are small and mat-forming, while others are larger with erect stems.

Coiling Fern:
*Young fern (**Dryopteris**) unfolding in early-June.*

8-14

9-

Iceberg:
*Carried southward by the Labrador Current icebergs drift
into northward-facing bays during April to June. Some run
aground and lie melting there well into July.*

8-15

10-1

10-1A

10-1B

10-2

11-1

11-2

1. ROSEROOT
(Sedum rosea)

May be found classed as a separate genus – *Rhodiola*. It is a fleshy-stemmed plant up to a foot or more in height and having several to many stems originating from a common rootstock. Leaves are fleshy, sessile, stubby (broadly ovate to triangular) and may be alternate or more densely foliated in the form of overlapping leaves spiralling up the stem. Flowers occur in terminal clusters and may be monoecious (separate male and female flowers on one plant) or dioecious (separate male and female plants). Male flowers are 4-petalled and yellow; female flowers are reddish-purple. The example shown is a mounded mass of male dioecious flowers found growing in mid-July at Watt's Point Calcareous Barrens.

1A.

An example of monoecious rose-root occurring at Watt's Point Calcarious Barrens in early-June, three years prior to the previous example. Note the dense, spiralling leaf arrangement; the waxy leaf surface; and the size of leaf increasing upwards along the stem. Note also the comparatively few 4-petalled, yellow, staminate flowers (compared with the previous example) and the reddish background matrix of pistillate (female) flowers.

1B.

An example of female dioecious roseroot, also occurring at Watt's Point Calcareous Barrens but in early-August of the year after example 1A. Note that the groups of 4 carpels joined at the base have, by this time of year, matured into seed-bearing follicles (seed cases which split along one side only). An example of seed-case remnant from the previous year's growth is also seen in the foreground.

2. ROSY STONECROP
(Sedum spurium)

A low-growing, prostrate and creeping species with thick, fleshy stems up to 3 inches high, bearing a terminal cluster of pink, 5-petalled, bell-shaped flowers having deeper red stigma and stamens projecting upwards from the central base of the flower. Leaves are fleshy, sessile, pointed-oval and bluntly toothed. The example shown is part of a large mat of these growing in early-August at the edge of a small cemetery terminating a rough, gravel road which more or less follows the north shoreline of Bay Bulls, south of St. John's.

11. SAXIFRAGE FAMILY
(Saxifragaceae)

Flowers usually having 5 petals and 5 sepals (sometimes 4 of each); 1 or 2 stamens per petal arise from the base of a 1–3 part ovary. A separate stigma occurs at the apex of each ovary part (carpel).

1. NAKED MITERWORT
(Mitella nuda)

Small, 5-petalled, greenish-white flowers on a thin leafless stem up to 8 inches tall. Sepals extend well beyond petals in the form of finely narrow tips having long lateral filaments. Low basal leaves are a rounded heart-shape with slightly uneven margins. The example shown was growing in mid-July at Watt's Point Calcareous Barrens. The more prominent leaves in the photograph are not those of *M. nuda*. These are seen somewhat out of focus near the bottom of the picture at the base of the flower stems.

2. MOUNTAIN SAXIFRAGE
(Saxifraga aizoides)

A low, creeping, mat-forming plant with narrow, alternating, fleshy leaves. Erect flower stems with the same leaf type rise

6–8 inches above the creeping stems and bear few-flowered terminal panicles of yellow-petalled flowers and nodding buds. Petals and sepals are of equal length. This plant is locally named "Man and Woman", perhaps comparing the flowering stems with the short mat-forming stems. The example shown was growing in late-July in a wet roadside ditch at Cow Head, a community enclave within Gros Morne National Park.

3. PURPLE SAXIFRAGE
(*Saxifraga oppositifolia*)
Relatively large, solitary, pale purple flowers at the tip of low, creeping stems. Petals overlap each other; are slightly reflexed at the tip; and are much larger than the sepals. The example shown was growing in mid-July at Watt's Point Calcareous Barrens. Creeping stems are mainly hidden by leaves of other low growth, such as the shiny, mottled willow leaves typical of the area.

4. MARSH GRASS-OF-PARNASSUS
(*Parnassia palustris*)
A single 5-petalled white flower atop a 6-10 inch stem. Basal leaves are stalked and spade-shaped. A lone spade-shaped leaf clasps the stem near its mid-point. Petals are paddle-shaped, longer than sepals, and have 7 prominent veins. The example shown was growing in late-August at Black Tickle on the Labrador Coast.

Some taxonomists treat Grass-of- Parnassus as a separate family – *Parnassiaceae*, because it has only 5 fertile stamens rather than 10 as in other Saxifrages. (The other stamen-like filaments –"staminoids"– are infertile and pronged into 2 or more tines). Others treat it as a genus of the Saxifrage Family and we have followed this practice. Examples of other members of this genus are:

4A. KOTZEBUE'S GRASS-OF-PARNASSUS
(*Parnassia kotzebuei*)

Basal leaves are spade-shaped but very short-stalked. Stem may be leafless or bear a small, sessile leaf near the base of the plant. Petals are the same length as sepals; do not have a paddle handle; and have only 3 prominent leaf-veins. The example shown was growing in mid-July at Watt's Point.

4B. SMALL-FLOWERED GRASS-OF-PARNASSUS
(*Parnassia parviflora*)
Basal leaves are eliptical, tapering to the tip. A stem leaf is present but sessile rather than clasping the stem and is strongly ascendant. Petals are longer than sepals and have 5 prominent veins. The example shown was growing in mid-July at The Arches Picnic Park on the coast just north of Gros Morne National Park.

5. SKUNK CURRANT
(*Ribes glandulosum*)
A sprawling woody shrub with erect racemes of white, pink-tinged, cup-shaped, 5-petalled flowers arising from leaf axils. Its petal tips are flared outwards. The calyx (fused sepals) and flower stalk are hairy. Leaves are palmate, toothed and distinctly 5-lobed. Fruit are drooping clusters of bristled, edible, red berries. The example shown was growing in late-May beside a gravel road serving summer cabins in the Deer Park Area off the Salmonier Line. The genus *Ribes* may sometimes be classed as a separate family – *Grossulariaceae* (Currant Family).

6. SWAMPY RED CURRANT
(*Ribes triste*)
A woody shrub similar to the foregoing, but with drooping racemes of dull reddish-purple, 5-petalled flowers with reflexed petal tips. Calyx and flower stalks may be smooth or with few hairs. Fruit are drooping clusters of smooth edible, red berries. The example shown was growing beside the James Callaghan Trail, Gros Morne National Park in early-June.

11-3

11-4

11-4A

11-4B

11-5

11-6

12-1

12-1A

Stephenville:
*The Abitibi-Price Paper Mill seen from Indian Head Park.
The harbour was made by U.S. Engineers when constructing
Ernest Harmon Air Force Base during World War II.*

12-2

12-3

12-4

12. ROSE FAMILY
(*Rosaceae*)

Named for the most widely known and most commonly cultivated member of the family, the rose, these are generally recognized by their 5 roundish petals and numerous stamens surrounding the centre of the flower. However, many variations exist, such as Canadian Burnet (*Sanguisorba canadensis*), an elongated flower spike covered with soft, white stamens, but having no petals; and Mountain Avens (*Dryas integrifolia*) having 8 petals.

1. MEADOWSWEET
(*Spiraea latifolia*)

An erect shrub, 2–3 ft. in height, usually occurring in extensive thickets. Many small 5-petalled, usually creamy-white flowers form compact pyramidal panicles at the extremity of each stem. Leaves are oval, alternate and toothed. The example shown was growing along the roadway entrance to the Sir Robert Bond Community Park at Whitbourne in mid-July. Flower clusters at the end of each stalk appear fuzzy due to the many stamens protruding from each flower. The white to pinkish-white variety is the most common.

1A.

A more deeply pink variety was found growing on the edge of a boggy area at the entrance to Murray's Pond Country Club on Portugal Cove Road, St. John's in August of the same year. Being more of a close-up photograph, the five petals of the individual flower and the numerous stamens are readily discernable.

2. WHITE QUEEN-OF-THE-PRAIRIE
(*Filipendula ulmaria*)

Erect red-tinged woody stems up to 5 ft. or more, bearing dense terminal clusters of creamy-white flowers. Lance-shaped leaves are pinnate and slightly lobed. Pairs of small, vestigial leaves also occur sporadically along the smooth stems. The example shown was growing in mid-July at Bowring Park, St. John's. This flower is sometimes also called "Meadowsweet".

3. PURPLE CHOKEBERRY
(*Aronia prunifolia*)

A woody shrub, up to 5 ft. high, with glossy, very finely toothed leaves. Flowers have 5 well-separated, oval petals and occur in terminal clusters. Petals and centre are both white. The example shown was growing in a narrow band of marsh edging a small stream at the western boundary of a cemetery at Stephenville in early July.

Ernest Harmon Air Force Base was constructed by American forces at Stephenville during World War II and continued to expand up to the early 50's. As was commonly the case, a civilian town developed alongside the military establishment. The airport, buildings and facilities were turned over to civilian use in 1966 and now form part of the Town of Stephenville.

4. CHUCKLEY PEARS
(*Amelanchier spp.*)

A woody shrub, up to 10 ft. high. Flowers have 5 oblong to linear, white, spreading, often twisted petals. Flowers occur in racemes throughout its branches, blooming before the leaves are fully grown. Leaves are alternate, pointed-oval to oblong, and finely to coarsely toothed. Glen Ryan's book – "Native Trees and Shrubs of Newfoundland and Labrador" – notes that there are 8 to 19 species variously recognized in eastern North America on the basis of minor differences, and that hybridization occurs making species identification rather difficult. The example shown was growing at the west end of Long Pond, St. John's in mid-June. The emergence of Chuckly Pear blossoms marks a step in the progress of Spring when river banks and forest edges are rampant with these blossoms.

5A. COMMON STRAWBERRY
(*Fragaria virginiana*)

5B. WOOD STRAWBERRY
(*Fragaria vesca*)

What a "common" little berry
But I love you more than most,
For I have you with my breakfast
As jam upon my toast.

As I savour your red sweetness
During winter's frosty days,
I remember early summer
With its warm sunny rays.

Leaves of *F. virginiana* are larger and rounded at the ends. *F. vesca* leaves are elongated and pointed. Also, the flowers of *virginiana* tend to remain below the leaves, while *vesca* flowers generally rise above them. Both of these pictures were taken in mid- to late-June, the former at Indianhead Park, Stephenville and the latter near the junction of Salmonier Line and the Trans-Canada Highway.

6. BAKE-APPLE/CLOUDBERRY
(*Rubus chamaemorus*)
A. Flower; B. Berry
These creeping plants bear solitary, white, usually 5-petalled, dioecious flowers and strongly wrinkled, palmate, 5-lobed, toothed leaves. They grow on most peat bogs throughout the province, berries ripening from mid-July in southern portions of the Island to late August in northern portions of Labrador. Berries are usually picked while still hard (being soft and squishy when ripe) and are stored in jars of water to ripen to their full juiciness. A Bake-apple Festival is held annually in the south coastal Labrador area (L'Anse au Clair – Red Bay), usually around the first week of August, combining garden parties, folk festivals, craft displays and other gala events with bake-apple picking .

The bake-apple berry picture was taken on the last day of August at Black Tickle, Labrador; being one of the many ports of call of the coastal vessel Northern Ranger on its scheduled round from Lewisporte to Nain. Crowberry branches are also seen in the picture.

7A. STEMLESS PLUMBOY
(*Rubus acaulis*)
A solitary, white, 5-petalled flower. Its 3-part wedge-shaped leaves are strongly veined, coarsely toothed, and broadly rounded at their extremity. The example shown was growing in early-July at Cape Spear, the most easterly point of Newfoundland.

7B. ARCTIC PLUMBOY
(*Rubus arcticus*)
A deep pink to purple 6-petalled, low-growing flower. Its petals are relatively long and narrow, extending beyond the pointed sepals. The 3-part leaves are wrinkled (deeply veined) and coarsely toothed. Note also the pink tubular central disc. Those shown were growing at Watt's Point in mid-July.

8. NEAT BLACKBERRY
(*Rubus elegantulus*)
These are perhaps the showiest of the raspberry-type flowers, having 6-8 flowers to a cluster. When formed, the berry is similar to a raspberry (each berry comprised of numerous "drupes") but is black rather then red when ripe. Main stems are 2–3 ft. horizontal or arching canes from which new growth arises each year. Leaves are palmate, usually with 3 wrinkled, pointed-oval leaflets. Stems bear intermittent small spines but are otherwise smooth. Those shown were growing beside Newfoundland Power's flume (penstock) carrying water to the Seal Cove hydro-electric generating plant. Occasional pin-holes in the penstock emit a fine spray providing a moisture laden climate throughout the growing season.

12-5A

12-5B

12-6B

12-6A

12-8

12-7A

12-7B

12-9

12-10

12-11

12-12

12-13

12-14

12-15

9. COMMON RASPBERRY
(*Rubus idaeus*)

A rather drab flower, generally going unnoticed until it ripens into a red berry. Note the well separated, small, white petals and the long, pointed, pale green sepals. Raspberries are usually one of the first growths to appear after a forest fire has decimated an area.

10. HAIRY PLUMBOY/GROUND RASPBERRY/DWARF RASPBERRY
(*Rubus pubescens*)

A small, single stem raspberry usually not exceeding one foot in height. Petals white but sometimes with a pinkish tinge. Normally found growing in sheltered woodland locations where at first glance it may be taken for a maple seedling. This one was growing in mid-July at Watt's Point Calcareous Barrens. Note the long, pointed, reflexed sepals.

11. CANADIAN BURNET/ BOTTLE BRUSH
(*Sanguisorba canadensis*)

The long stamens associated with the flower spike give the bottle-brush appearance. The lower flowers of each spike open first and go to seed first. The upper portion of most of the spikes shown have not yet flowered, while one of the spikes has already completely matured to brown seeds. This specimen was about 4 ft. tall growing in Jack's Pond Provincial Park, near Arnold's Cove on the Isthmus of the Avalon Peninsula. Other local names given to this flower, according to Rouleau, are Caribou-feed, Indian Tobacco, and Marsh Lily.

12. THREE-TOOTHED CINQUEFOIL
(*Potentilla tridentata*)

A small white flower belonging to the "cinquefoil" sub-family even though it has 3-part leaves. These leaves are shiny, close to the ground and turn a brilliant red in the fall. The name "three-toothed" refers to the three teeth or serrations at the extremity of each leaflet. The flower stalk rises 2–6 inches above the basal leaves and is branched to separately support each of the 3–10 or more flowers. Smaller pointed leaflets occur at each flower-stalk junction. The photograph was taken in late August on the summit of Mt. Scio. (Colloquial name – Simple Tea).

13. ROUGH CINQUEFOIL
(*Potentilla norvegica*)

Another "cinquefoil" with 3-part leaves. This one is taller, up to 2 feet in height, and with yellow flowers. The petals are about the same length as the pointed sepals, and the leaves are coarsely toothed throughout their margin. The example shown was growing in late August on the isthmus of the Avalon Peninsula, at the junction of the Southern Harbour Road with the Trans Canada Highway.

14. COMB CINQUEFOIL
(*Potentilla pectinata*)

Yellow 5-petalled flowers atop an erect stem. Each flower arises from a leaf axil and is closely backed by an upper stem leaf. Sepals are as long as, or longer, than petals. Leaves are alternate and pinnate. Lower leaves are long-stalked with 2–4 pairs of long-oval, round-toothed leaflets and a similar terminal leaflet. Upper stem leaves have shorter stalks and 3 leaflets. Some taxonomists consider this to be an eastern sub-species or variety of Prairie Cinquefoil (*P. pensylvanica*). The example shown was 1–1$\frac{1}{2}$ ft. high, growing at Black Tickle, Labrador in late August.

15. SILVERY CINQUEFOIL
(*Potentilla argentea*)

A low, multi-stemmed, branching cinquefoil with 5-petalled yellow flowers occurring in terminal clusters or cymes. Leaves occur in groups of 3–5 narrow, wedge-shaped, terminally-lobed leaflets whorled at branch junctures. Stems and the underside of leaves are covered with a white pubescence. The example shown was growing near the CBC Building, Prince Philip Drive, St. John's in mid-July.

16. SHRUBBY CINQUEFOIL
(*Potentilla fruticosa*)
A shrubby plant with woody stems to a height of 2–3 ft. Leaflets are small, narrow, almost linear and untoothed. Being a hardy, well-flowered species, it has been domesticated in many gardens either as an accent plant or for hedging. The specimen shown was growing on the shoreline of Indian Arm Pond in mid-July. (Colloquial name "Goldwithy).

16A.
An example of the same species at a much more diminutive scale found growing at Watt's Point Calcareous Barrens, also in mid-July.

Glen Ryan, in his book "Native Trees And Shrubs Of Newfoundland And Labrador", notes that Shrubby Cinquefoil may vary in height from 0.2 –1.3 m and is less commonly found "...on dry rocky barrens and limestone talus." This is probably such an example.

17. COMMON CINQUEFOIL
(*Potentilla simplex*)
A prostrate cinquefoil with flowers and leaves arising separately from runners. Leaves are palmate with 5 leaflets, toothed only at the end of the leaflets, as shown in the upper right of the photograph. The example shown was growing at MUN Botanic Park, Nagle's Hill, St. John's in mid-July.

18. MARSH CINQUEFOIL
(*Potentilla palustris*)
Found in marshy locations as the name implies, the flower has six short, deep red to purple petals and long pointed, brownish sepals which extend well beyond the petals. The fruit is strawberry-like, but hard and

dry and is seen in the process of formation in the photograph, taken at Black Tickle, Labrador, at the end of August.

Black Tickle is a fishing community south of Hamilton Inlet on the coast of Labrador, having a permanent population of 40 to 50 families, but a summer population well in excess of this, resulting from an influx of fishermen, many with their families, who have traditionally fished these coastal waters on a seasonal basis, some for several generations.

19. DWARF CINQUEFOIL
(*Potentilla canadensis*)
A prostrate cinquefoil with flowers and leaves arising separately from rooting nodes on a purplish, hairy, creeping stem. Flowers have 4–5 yellow petals, twice as long as the sepals. The flower stalk is thin, recumbent and finely hairy. Leaves are long-stalked with 5 wedge-shaped leaflets, toothed on the outer edge. The example shown was growing in early-August on the mossy bank of a small, trickling stream beside a cart track extending onwards from the end of a roadway parallelling the North shoreline of Bay Bulls. Note that it has 4, rather than 5 petals.

20. SILVERWEED
(*Potentilla anserina*)
Another form of prostrate cinquefoil growing by runners from which flowers and leaves extend separately from nodes. Its leaves are shiny and comprised of multiple pairs of toothed leaflets. It is quite tolerant of maritime conditions and is often found growing at the back of coastal beaches where beach stones grade into soil. The example shown was growing in early-July at Indianhead Park, Stephenville.

20A.
Silverweed in fruit at Black Tickle, Labrador, early-September.

12-16

12-16A

12-17

12-18

12-19

12-20

12-20A

12-21

12-22

12-23

12-24

12-25

Green Gardens Trail:
A view from the Trail, southwards along the coast in Gros Morne National Park. (Also see text of 15-1A, page 25)

12-26

21. ENGLISH CINQUEFOIL/ TRAILING TORMENTIL
(*Potentilla anglica*)

Relatively large yellow flowers having 4 or 5 broad petals. Flowers occur singly along slender purplish runners. Pinnate leaves vary from 3 leaflets similar to those of (*P. tridentata*,) to 5 palmate leaflets. The example shown was growing at Watt's Point Calcareous Barrens in early June.

22. LADY'S MANTLE
(*Alchemilla vulgaris*)

Usually occurring as prostrate runners but sometimes upright, it is easily recognized by its large 6- to 9-lobed palmate, toothed leaves. Branching flower stems also arise from the runners and have joined pairs of fan-shaped, lobed and toothed leaves at branch junctions. The small flowers occur in greenish-yellow clusters, each flower having five pointed sepals but no petals. The stem is quite hairy. New growth may occur from rootstock branches formed in the previous year. Seed formation is usually apomictic (not requiring pollination). However, pollination may occur by the matured stigma curving backwards to touch the pollen on the later-maturing stamens (protogyny). This plant demonstrates how nature often provides a variety of ways by which plants may reproduce themselves, enabling continued propagation under changing environmental conditions. Nevertheless we humans insist on testing their perseverence to the limit, and frequently beyond. The example shown was growing in a newly developing summer cabin area off the Salmonier Line in late May.

23. AGRIMONY
(*Agrimonia striata*)

Yellow 5-petalled flowers densely grouped in a long, slender, terminal spike and on shorter racemes arising from leaf axils of the upper leaves. Its compound leaves alternate up the stem and are comprised of 3 large, long-oval, toothed, sharply pointed, termi-nal leaflets with pairs of large and small similar leaflets interspersed along the remaining length of leaf stalk. The upper stem of the plant is noticeably hairy. The example shown was about 18 inches high and growing in late-July alongside Green Gardens Trail in Gros Morn National Park.

24. YELLOW AVENS
(*Geum alleppicum*)

Found in moist, sheltered and shady locations where it may grow to 3 ft. or more. Note its hairy stem and 5 round, well separated, yellow petals which are longer than the sepals. The 3-lobed, wedge-shaped, sharply-toothed leaves are variable and may be stalked or sessile with pairs of broad stipules at the stem juncture. Several stages of progress in fruit production are evident in the photograph taken in early July.

25. WATER AVENS
(*Geum rivale*)

Flower heads nodding on hairy purple stems rise from broad, 3-part, basal leaves toothed at the extremities. Pale yellow petals are cupped by purple sepals of the same length so that only a little of the petals is noticeable, thus giving an overall purplish appearance. Usually found in wet soil conditions, these were growing at Watt's Point Calcareous Barrens in mid-July. We have seen this flower at the same stage of maturity a month or more earlier on the Port au Port Peninsula, 300 km due south.

26. MOUNTAIN AVENS
(*Dryas integrafolia*)

An 8-petalled, creamy-yellow, low-growing flower – the floral emblem of the Northwest Territories. The flowers arise separately from prostrate woody stems bearing small, narrow, evergreen, leathery, untoothed leaves, not visible in the photograph. Between mid-June and mid-July these flowers abound along the old roadway through Watt's Point Calcareous Barrens. Vehicles seldom travel this roadway because bridge crossings have fallen into disrepair thus further protecting the area as an ecological preserve.

27. NORTHEASTERN ROSE
(*Rosa nitida*)

A deep-pink, fragrant rose with sepals shorter than petals. Flowers usually occur singly, but may sometimes be in few-flowered clusters. The stem is densely covered with bristles which are red on new stems. Longer spikes or spines occur more sparsely on the stem. Leaves are alternate and pinnate with 7–9 finely toothed, pointed-elliptical leaflets. Stipules fringe the base of each leaf stalk. The example shown was less than 2 ft. high and was growing in mid-August on the edge of a marsh near Seal Cove River, Conception Bay.

28. VIRGINIA ROSE
(*Rosa virginiana*)

A pink, slender-stemmed rose with thorns and bristles absent or occurring only on the lower portion of the stem. Note the reddish stem, leaf-stalks and stipules. The example shown was growing in mid-August near Seal Cove River, upstream from the Conception Bay Highway.

29. DOG ROSE
(*Rosa rubrifolia*)

Petals pink at the extremities but shading quickly to white at the centre. Sepals are long and narrow, much longer than petals. The stem is deep purple and smooth with few, if any, spines or bristles. Foliage is a dark dullish green, tinged red along the sharp-toothed margins. Note the long sepals extending well beyond the tip of the buds, and the curled petal tips giving the appearance of petals being pointed. The example shown was growing in late-August between Long Pond and the Health Sciences Centre, St. John's.

30. WRINKLED ROSE
(*Rosa rugosa*)

A pink-petaled rose arising from sturdy, bristly stems interspersed with longer thorns. The finely toothed leaves are thick and appear to be wrinkled as a result of leaf veins being deeply incised into the leaf structure. The example shown was growing in mid-August near Bay Roberts on the west side of Conception Bay.

13. PEA FAMILY
(*Leguminosae*)

Flowers of this family are generally irregular in appearance and function, but are typically bilaterally symmetrical (like a butterfly, and hence the alternative family name – *papillionaceae*). Most have 5 petals. The bottom two are fused to form a "keel" containing the pistil and usually 10 stamens. The top petal is enlarged forming a wide "collar" or "banner". The side petals are called "wings". In some instances, as in clovers, the flower head is composed of a cluster of many small flowers.

1. GARDEN LUPINE
(*Lupinus polyphyllus*)

Tall spikes of pea-type flowers in whorls atop sturdy, green to purplish stems up to 4 ft. high. They are common garden escapes throughout the island part of the province, usually having reverted to blue or purple colours from the initial planting of multi-coloured crosses, although white and pink colours are often found mingled among them. Leaves are long stalked, terminating in a palmate whorl of 9 to 12 or more untoothed, lance-shaped leaflets. One of life's simple but profound pleasures is derived from observing morning dew or raindrops cupped by each leaf as sparkling crystal globules. The flowers shown were growing in mid-July in a vacant field fronting on Kenmount Road in

12-27 12-28

12-29 12-30

Health Sciences Centre, St. John's:
A general hospital providing acute care, teaching and medical research facilities.

13-1

13-2

13-3

13-5

13-6

13-4

13-7

13-8

the outskirts of St. John's. Unfortunately it was mid-morning and any dew accumulation that there might have been had evaporated.

2. WHITE SWEET CLOVER
(*Melilotus alba*)
Racemes of white clover-type flowers at the extremity of tall multi-branched stems growing to a height of 5 feet or more. These were growing in a vacant lot near the junction of Water and Waldegrave Streets in St. John's in early-August. Note the 3-part, finely toothed leaves arising from the smooth stem.

3. YELLOW SWEET CLOVER
(*Melilotus officinalis*)
Similar to White Sweet Clover (*M. alba*) but with yellow flowers. These were growing in late-July along the roadside leading to the Trout River camping park, Gros Morne National Park. The water in the background of the photograph is Lower Trout River Pond. To the left, bathed in sunlight, are the lower slopes of Table Mountain.

4. WHITE CLOVER
(*Trifolium repens*)
A round flower head composed of many pea-like white flowers growing on 3-9 inch stalks arising from runners. 3-Part oval leaves arise separately from runners and are usually marked with a pale crescent as seen in the photograph, taken in mid-July alongside the road leading to the beach at Topsail Head, Conception Bay.

5. RED CLOVER
(*Trifolium pratense*)
The red or pink flowerhead has the same form and composition as White Clover (*T. repens*), but the stem is slightly hairy and may be branched to support two or more flowerheads. Three-part leaves are elliptical and pointed, with separate leaf-stalks arising at stem junctions and at the base of each flowerhead. Leaflets are also marked

with a pale crescent or triangle. The photograph was taken in early-June at the western end of Long Pond, St. John's.

6. ALSIKE CLOVER
(*Trifolium hybridum*)
Frequently sown as a forage crop, this clover has become a common escape from pastures and grows wild in fields and along the roadside. The flowerhead is comprised of many white to pinkish pea-like flowers. The stem is sturdy and usually branched to support two or more flowerheads. Leaves are coarser and more strongly veined than the previous two clovers and have no pale markings.

7. YELLOW CLOVER/HOP CLOVER
(*Trifolium agrarium*)
A yellow flowerhead, similar in form to the previous clovers , but having a more frequently branching stem. The 3-part leaves are elliptical, unmarked, and arise at regular intervals along the stem, but do not occur at the base of the flowerhead. The example shown was growing in mid-July at Whitbourne.

8. BLACK MEDICK
(*Medicago lupulina*)
The flower, 3-part oval leaves and branching habit are similar to Hop Clover, but note the slightly hairy and angular or ridged stem; the tiny sharp point at the end of each leaflet; and the clump of curved, black seeds which may be mistaken as an infestation of small grubs. The example shown was growing near Stephenville in early-August.

9. BIRDFOOT TREFOIL
(*Lotus corniculatus*)
A circle or part-circle of yellow pea-type flowers at the end of branched stems. 5-Part leaves have 3 leaflets at the extremity and two at the base of the leaf stem. The latin name indicates that it is "horned", probably referring to the flower's upper petal which curves sharply upwards from the "snout"

formed by the other petals. The name "bird-foot" seems to bear a rather tenuous relationship with the flower. The picture was taken in early July at Terra Nova National Park.

10. BEACH PEA
(*Lathyrus japonicus*)
A cluster of pale pink to purple pea-type flowers on a slightly hairy flower stalk. The paired parts of the flower petals may be of quite different shades as shown in the photograph. Leaves consist of paired or alternating oval leaflets; a pair of tendrils extending from the end of the leaf stalk; and a pair of arrow-shaped leaflets (stipules) at the junction with the main stem. The flowers shown were growing at Indian Head Park, Stephenville in mid-July. The channel entry from St. George's Bay into Port Harmon separates the park from the mountainous terrain of the Indian Head Range, the shoreward portion of which contains marble deposits.

11. ST. JOHN OXYTROPIS
(*Oxytropis johannensis*)
Prostrate leaf and flower stalks extend radially from the root area. Magenta and white pea-type flowers clustered at the end of slightly hairy stalks give the plant a wreath-like appearance. Leaves are pinnate with many paired or alternating leaflets occurring quite thickly along the leaf-stalk. Leaflets tend to be curled in along the edges. This is a close relative of the notoriously poisonous Locoweed (*Oxytropis lambertii*) found in southern parts of the Prairie Provinces. The picture, taken in mid-July at Watt's Point, shows only about 1/8 or 45° of the plant's overall 3 ft. diameter formation.

12. CROWN VETCH
(*Coronilla varia*)
A cluster of pink and white pea-type flowers on long, creeping stems with pinnate leaves. A clump of this was growing in early-September at the edge of a clearing alongside the road at Flat Bay, a small community south of St. Georges on the west coast of the Island. A nearby large limestone deposit is presently being quarried for export.

13. COW/TUFTED/BIRD VETCH
(*Vicia cracca*)
A climbing plant commonly found tangled among foliage at the edge of pastures and roadways. The flowers may vary from pale blue to purple and are in the form of a one-sided spike of pea-like flowers. Leaves are pinnate with tendrils at the end. The photograph was taken in mid-July at the edge of the old railway route through Whitbourne.

14. FALSE LUPINE/YELLOW PEA
(*Thermopsis montana*)
Yellow pea-type flowers growing from upper-leaf axils, forming a raceme atop sturdy, slightly hairy stems up to 3 ft. or more in height. Leaves are stalked, alternate and have 3 broad-oval, untoothed leaflets. A pair of broad leaf-like stipules occur at the base of each leaf-stalk. The example shown was growing in profusion on a large vacant lot west of Belvedere Cemetery, St. John's in late-June.

13-9

13-10

13-11

13-12

13-13

Flat Bay:
Gypsum, used in the manufacture of cement, is quarried at Flat Bay and trucked to a cement plant in Corner Brook.

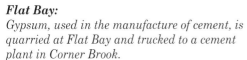

13-14

14-1

15-1

15-1A

15-2

Black Tickle, Labrador:
*Decline of cod stocks,
resulting in the "Cod
Moritorium" of 1993 – ?,
indicates that this scene
(1989) is unlikely to be
repeated for some
considerable time. (See text
12–18, page 20).*

14. FLAX FAMILY
(Linaceae)

Rouleau's List of Newfoundland Plants contains reference to only two species of one genus of this family being found in Newfoundland: *Linum catharticum* – a white-flowered species having small, paired, oval leaves; and *Linum usitatissimum* – a blue flowered species having narrow, alternate leaves. We have only seen the latter species as described below:

1. COMMON FLAX
(*Linum usitatissimum*)
Small, blue, cupped flowers on smooth, slender, branching stems up to 1 ft. with a reclining tendency. The 5 petals overlap and are cupped at the base by 5 green sepals. Leaves are alternate, unstalked, narrow-lanceolate, straight-edged, and have 3 parallel veins. The example shown was growing in our backyard in late-September and probably originated from birdseed scattered during wintertime.

15. GERANIUM/CRANESBILL FAMILY
(*Geraniaceae*)

5-Part, radially symmetrical flowers on slender, usually branching stems. Leaves may be palmate, pinnate or double-pinnate. When fruiting, the style and stigma elongate forming a long-beaked seed case, the basis for the "cranesbill" name.

1. HERB-ROBERT
(*Geranium robertianum*)
Usually paired, pink to magenta, 5-petalled flowers arising on long stalks from leaf axils. Sepals are noticeably hairy and remain partly closed, cupping the lower portion of the petals. Leaves are paired and pinnate with 3–5 deeply lobed leaflets. These were growing at Long Point on the Port-au-Port Peninsula in late-June. Note the reddish stigma protruding from the end of the "cranesbill"; the deep red stalks and stem; and the small bracts at the flower stalk juncture.

1A.
A white-flowered variety found growing beside Green Gardens Trail, Gros Morne National Park, in mid-July. Note that stalks and stem in this instance are more green than red, and appear to be less hairy than the pink variety.

Green Gardens Trail leads northward from the road to Trout River; first over barren "moonscape" at the base of The Tablelands; then through mixed fir and spruce forest to open grassland along a raised coastal plateau; returning by way of a trail following a stream arising in The Tablelands. To do this walk in a leisurely way it is best to camp overnight at one of the remote camping sites along the grassland section of the trail.

2. MEADOW CRANESBILL
(*Geranium pratense*)
Clusters of blue to mauve flowers with broad, overlapping petals on slightly hairy and sticky stalks. Deep purple anthers give the flower a peppered appearance. Flowers of this species are "protandrous", the stamens mature and wither before the stigma matures. This avoids self-pollination within each flower. But pollination between flowers of the same plant may still occur, as flowers in the same cluster mature at different times. Leaves are palmate, usually with seven main lobes. These are commonly found as garden escapes originating from more exotic crosses which have reverted to form. The example shown was growing in late-August beside our house.

16. TOUCH-ME-NOT FAMILY
(*Balsaminaceae*)

Leafy, branching, succulent-stemmed plants bearing pendulent, bilaterally symmetrical flowers on long flower stalks arising from leaf axils. Most species are tropical. One species of the genus *Impatiens* is a common houseplant - Busy Lizzie (*I. wallerana*). Other species which occur as wildflowers in Newfoundland are also of the same genus.

1. SPOTTED TOUCH-ME-NOT/JEWELWEED
(*Impatiens capensis*)

A deep-yellow, orange spotted, bilaterally symmetrical flower, usually hanging in pairs on long stalks arching from leaf axils. It has 5 petals, the lower 2 forming a broad lip; 2 smaller side petals; and a larger, hood-forming upper petal. These petals are fused behind the sepals, forming a bulbous spur which terminates in a thin tail turning sharply forward. The flower stem is smooth, succulent, branching, and may grow to 4 ft. or more in height. Leaves are pointed-oval, toothed, short-stalked and alternate. A paler yellow, less spotted form (*Impatiens pallida*) is also noted in Rouleau's List, but is less common and we have not yet seen it. The example shown is from an extensive mass of these plants growing along a 100 ft. length of ditch by the side of the road on Topsail Hill in early-September.

2. PINK TOUCH-ME-NOT/ HIMALAYAN BALSAM
(*Impatiens glandulifera*)

A somewhat larger pink flower, having a smaller spur tail but the same petal structure as *I. capensis*. Flowers are clustered at the ends of purple flower-stalks. One flower blooms at a time resulting in a long period of bloom. Buds, flowers, seed pods, and pod remnants after seed discharge, may be found on a plant at the same time. The thick, succulent, purplish main stem may reach 5 ft. or more in height and has a thickened light-green sheath at branch junctions. Leaves are pointed-elliptical, edged with small barbs, conspicuously veined (main leaf veins often being purplish), and are either paired or in whorls of 3. Three examples are shown:

2A.
Shows the overall size of a plant, its thick main stem, strongly branched nature, purplish veined leaves, and single flower blooming per cluster. This was one of many growing in late-September along a 200 ft. length of ditch beside the gravel-surfaced laneway extension of Oxen Pond Road alongside a farm on the western slope of Mount Scio in St. John's.

2B.
Shows flowers from bud to empty seed pod (dehisced) on a plant growing in early-August in an untended backyard on Gilbert Street in downtown St. John's. Leaf structure and form, including small barbs along the leaf edge, are clearly shown.

2C.
A more detailed picture of the flower, showing the cluster arrangement. Note also the form of seed capsule to the right of the photograph. When mature, a light touch will trigger the capsule into sudden opening and forceful seed ejection.

16-1

Winterholme:
Built in 1905 for Sir Marmaduke Winter, a businessman and politician of the time, Winterholme is now operated as a tourist home by the present owner.

Kimberly Row:
Houses typical of those built in downtown St. John's after the Great Fire of 1892.

16-2A

16-2B

16-2C

Bay Bulls:
A community of about 1,000 population at the southern outskirts of St. John's.

17-1

18-1

17-1A

18-2

18-3

17. MALLOW FAMILY
(*Malvaceae*)

Most members of this family are tropical plants such as hibiscus and cotton plants. Hollyhock is also a member of the family and is grown in many local gardens, but is not considered to be a wildflower in this province, not having naturalized to any significant extent or to have become a common "escape". Rouleau's List of Newfoundland Plants includes only two species of the family – Musk Mallow (*Malva moschata*) and Round-leaved Mallow (*Malva neglecta*). Flowers are radially symmetrical with 5 broad showy petals, 5 sepals, and numerous stamens joined at the base forming a sheath or tube around the style of the pistil. Leaves are usually palmately lobed (like a maple leaf), sometimes deeply divided.

1. MUSK MALLOW
(*Malva moschata*)

Five pink, white or mauve, triangular shaped petals with slightly ragged outer edges. A sturdy, projecting, central pistil is surrounded by numerous stamens. Flowers are 1-inch or more in diameter and occur in terminal clusters or singly on stalks arising from leaf axils. Alternate leaves are palmate but finely divided. The example shown was growing in Mid-July among an extensive coverage of these plants along an old property line leading towards the north shoreline of Bay Bulls.

1A.

An example of pink Musk Mallow blooming in early-September near the east end of Long Pond, St. John's.

18. ST. JOHN'S-WORT FAMILY
(*Hypericaceae*)

Although there are several genera in the family, only one genus – *Hypericum* has species occurring in this province. Plants of this genus are radially symmetrical; have yellow flowers with 5 petals, 5 sepals, and with numerous stamens surrounding a central pistil having either a 3- or 5-part style. Leaves are usually paired, oval to elliptical, sessile (unstalked), and have untoothed edges.

1. COMMON ST. JOHN'S-WORT
(*Hypericum perforatum*)

A branching, bushy plant up to 2 ft. or more high, with terminal clusters of yellow, narrow-petalled flowers having a prominent central spray of stamens. Numerous paired, narrow-elliptical leaves give the plant its bushy appearance. The example shown was growing in late-September beside Higgin's Line, near Confederation Building, St. John's.

2. CANADIAN ST. JOHN'S-WORT
(*Hypericum canadense*)

A yellow, small-flowered, slender-stemmed species growing to a height of 8 to 18 inches. Its few sparsely-leafed branches have long and very narrow paired leaves. The example shown was growing in late-July in a marsh near Seal Cove River. Note the prominent red-brown, urn-shaped seed capsules and sepals not quite as long as the petals.

3. NORTHERN ST. JOHN'S-WORT
(*Hypericum boreale*)

A small-flowered species, similar to *H. canadense*, but has paired, broadly oval, 3–5 nerved leaves and a reclining lower stem. Note that the stamens are fewer and less prominent. The example shown was growing in a marsh near Whitbourne in mid-August.

19. VIOLET FAMILY
(*Violaceae*)

Low growing plants with round- to heart-shaped long-stalked leaves. Flowers are 5-parted, with 5 stamens and a central pistil. The 5 petals are bilaterally symmetrical, the lower petal typically being longer and extending backwards to form a blunt spur.

1. FIELD PANSY
(*Viola arvensis*)

A low-growing creamy-white violet with flowers on leafless stalks arising from leaf axils. The lower petal is broad and generally heart-shaped, tinged yellow, and purple- streaked towards the centre. The other petals are oval and may be tinged purple on the outer edge. Leaves are spatulate with bluntly toothed edges and have three-pronged or otherwise long-lobed stipules (smaller leaf-like parts at the base of a leaf stalk). Rouleau's List Of Newfoundland Plants refers to this as an introduced species. The example shown was growing in our back yard in mid-July and is probably descended from pansies planted 20 years earlier, but now reverted to their natural unhybridized state. (Its proper reference may therefore be: Wild Pansy – *Viola tricolour*).

2. KIDNEY-LEAVED VIOLET
(*Viola renifolia*)

A small white-petalled violet on a separate smooth green stem. The upper pair of petals are elliptical and tend to be somewhat reflexed. The bottom or lip petal is brown-veined, sometimes quite heavily so as in the example shown, and is broader and longer than the other petals. Leaves are kidney shaped, slightly toothed, and grow in a basal rosette to the same height as the flower on conspicuously hairy stalks. The example shown was growing in mid-June at Indian Arm Pond where there was quite a large patch growing in moist soil along the edge of a short trail leading to a boat-launching site. They are small and easily overlooked, but once noticed, close inspection is memorably revealing of their fragile natural beauty.

3. NORTHERN WHITE VIOLET
(*Viola palens*)

A white petalled flower similar to *V. renifolia* except that the upper and lateral petals are round to ovate, and the bottom petal is purple-veined and shorter than the others. Leaves are short-stemmed and more heart shaped than kidney shaped. The example shown was growing in early June in a forest area near Lomond, Gros Morne National Park. Seed in these flowers is commonly produced by self-pollination occurring in unopened flowers (cleistogamy).

4. NORTHERN BLUE VIOLET
(*Viola septentrionalis*)

Blue to deep purple petals, the lower 3 petals having short bristly hairs at the base (bearded). The lower petal extends backwards forming a quite noticeable blunt spur. Flowers are on separate stems rising above the leaves to a height of 6 inches or more. Leaves are heart-shaped with the lobes of the heart closed around the junction with the leaf stalk. The underside of leaves are purplish and leaf stalks are quite hairy. The example shown was growing in early-June in a grassy field atop low cliffs on the south side of Rocky Harbour.

Rocky Harbour is a municipal enclave in Gros Morne National Park and is the commercial and service centre for the population of the sub-region encompassed by the Park.

19-1

19-2

19-3

19-4

Rocky Harbour:
A *municipal enclave (Population, 1,200) in Gros Morne National Park, it is the commercial and service centre for the population of the sub-region encompassed by the Park.*

19-5

19-6

19-7

20-1

Gros Morne:
*Seen from the highway through Gros Morne National Park. it
is the second highest prominence on the Island of
Newfoundland, having an elevation of 2,644 ft. (806 m).*

20-2

5. ALPINE MARSH VIOLET
(Viola palustris)

A small, pale-violet, separately stemmed flower. Its lower 3 petals have deep-purple veining at the base, most prominent in the middle petal. Note the "bearding" at the base of the two lateral petals. Leaves are a rounded heart shape with a distinct "notch" at the junction with the leaf-stalk. The example shown was growing atop Gros Morne in the latter part of July.

The day we planned to climb the mountain turned out to be a beautiful, sunny day. The hike to the base of the mountain begins along a rising trail through mature balsam fir forest with moss and fern ground cover; then crosses a plateau of scrub trees and heath to a brook skirting the base of the mountain. Removing our footwear and dabbling our feet in the cold mountain stream was a sensuously pleasant experience. Even more soothing was the soft, feathery pliancy of the underwater moss-covered rocks against the soles of our feet. Rejuvenated, we commenced the ascent up a talus slope to the top of Gros Morne.

6. MARSH BLUE VIOLET
(Viola cuculata)

A small, purplish-blue violet, its lower petal shorter than the others. Lateral petals each have a clump of white hair-like projections at their base (bearded). The flower rises above the heart-shaped leaves on a separate flower stalk.

There was a heavy mist over the area on the morning this picture was taken and everything was covered with dew. The example shown was 3–4 inches tall, growing in mid-June on a wet part of lawn fronting one of the cabins at "The Governor's" on the Salmonier Line.

7. SWEET VIOLET
(Viola odorata)

A separately stemmed flower with deep red-violet petals. The lower petal is blunt or straight-edged rather than pointed-ovate and is "bearded". The flower rises to about the same height as the deeply notched heart-shaped leaves. The example shown was growing at Watt's Point Calcareous Barrens in mid-July.

20. EVENING PRIMROSE/ WILLOWHERB FAMILY
(Onagraceae)

Tubular, usually 4-petalled flowers with the same number of sepals as petals and 1–2 stamens per petal. A 4-lobed cross-shaped stigma is typical of the family. Flowers may occur in spikes or as single flowers in leaf axils.

1. SMALL FLOWERED EVENING PRIMROSE
(Oenothera parviflora)

A thickly leaved spike of yellow, 4-petalled flowers emerging from axils of the upper leaves on a usually unbranched stem. Grows to 3 or 4 ft. under ideal soil and exposure conditions, but to less than 1 ft. under adverse conditions. Buds are long, reddish and with distinctively spreading sepal tips. Sepals are fully reflexed when in bloom. The example shown was growing in early-July at Indian Head Park, Stephenville.

2. COMMON EVENING PRIMROSE
(Oenothera biennis)

Similar to *O. parviflora*, except that the stem is usually branched; flowering spikes are not as leafy; the stem is reddish; little leaves (stipules) occur at the leaf axils. Buds are pale green, more ascendent, and with smaller, less spreading sepal tips then in *O. parviflora*. The example shown was growing in mid-September beside the driveway to Murray's Pond Country Club on the outskirts of St. John's.

3. SUNDROPS
(*Oenothera perennis*)
Flowers are smaller than *O. parviflora or O. biennis*; petals are more obviously veined and less overlapping; and seed capsules are strongly ribbed. The example shown was growing in mid-July at Indian Head Park, Stephenville.

3A.
A lower-growing specimen (possibly a variety of *O. fruticosa*) found growing in mid-August at Thorburn Lake, south of Terra Nova National Park. It has leathery, round-tipped leaves and only a few terminal flowers. Note the large 4-part stigma.

4. FIREWEED
(*Epilobium angustifolium*)
A single long raceme of pink to rose-coloured 4-petalled flowers atop a 3-5 foot stem. Stem sometimes branched and secondary flower racemes may arise from upper leaf axils. A 4-part white stigma projects from the flower on a rather long style. Leaves are long, untoothed, lance-shaped, sharply pointed and occur spirally up the stem. Seed cases are long, slender, reddish-purple, strongly ascendant capsules. The example shown was growing in early-August at the foot of Mt. Scio, behind the Health Sciences Centre, St. John's.

5. NORTHERN WILLOW HERB
(*Epilobium glandulosum*)
Small, pink, 4-petalled flowers extending from leaf axils on elongated ovaries which eventually become long seed capsules. Petals are notched. Paired, sessile or short-stalked, finely-toothed leaves are pointed-ovate on the lower portion of the purple, 4-angled, usually unbranched stem. Upper leaves tend to be more lance-shaped. The stigma may or may not be clearly 4-lobed. The example shown was about 2 ½ feet tall, growing in my back yard in late-July.

5A.
A much-branched, green-stemmed specimen (probably *Var. adenocaulon*) with flowers in terminal clusters projecting from tight whorls of small, lance-shaped, finely toothed leaves. Also note the stiffly rising green seed pods and the heart-shaped, broad-based, round-tipped stem leaves. It was growing in a damp spot along Green Gardens Trail, Gros Morne National Park in late-July.

6. MARSH WILLOWHERB
(Epilobium palustre)
Very narrow, mostly paired, strongly ascendant, untoothed leaves on a thin, erect stem up to 18 inches high. Note the long, thin seed capsules and small white (sometimes pink) flowers. There are a number of recognized varieties of this species. The example shown is probably *Var. oliganthum* (few flowered). It was growing in mid-August at Southwest Pond, Salmonier Line.

7. STECKER'S WILLOWHERB
(*Epilobium steckerianum*)
A short, square-stemmed willowherb, sometimes exceeding 1 foot in height. Leaves pointed-ovate to lanceolate; sessile and rounded at the base; finely toothed; upper leaves strongly ascending and overlapping. Pink, 4-petalled, notched flowers arise from axils of the upper leaves. The example shown was growing on the bank of a small brook crossing the road to the Cape Norman Lighthouse at the northern extremity of the Great Northern Peninsula.

The flower is named for its discoverer, Adolph Stecker, a Moravian missionary in Labrador in the late 19th century. The Moravians were unsuccessful in their first attempt to establish a mission near Hopedale, Labrador in 1752, but later established missions at Nain (1771), Okak (1776), Hopedale (1782), Hebron (1830), Zoar (1866), Ramah (1871), Makkovik (1896), Killinek (1905). The latter site is located at the northernmost extremity of Labrador.

20-3A

20-3

20-4

20-5

20-5A

20-6

20-7

Moravian Church:
The Moravian Mission Church at Nain, Labrador, established 1771.

20-8

21-2

21-1A

21-1B

21-3

8. ENCHANTER'S NIGHTSHADE
(Circaea alpina)

Shiny specks ashiver in a shady nook!
Dare we creep nearer for a closer look?
With bated breath we silently sink
slowly to our knees.
Surely those are fairies at play
among the trees!
Suddenly a shaft of sun
lights up the little glade.
With camera poised, the shutter clicks,
another slide is made.
Did we really capture fairies
on our film for all to see?
Imagine if we did, what a wonder it would be.
The picture shows the shiny specks
above a leafy bower.
By magical enchantment
each one became a flower!
Magic and enchantment
abound in every bushy clump.
What's that hiding in the shadow
by the old tree stump?

Differing from other members of the family, this is a small white 2-part flower (2 deeply notched petals, 2 sepals and 2 stamens) on 1–3 sparsely flowered, terminal spikes seen in the photograph rising above the clump of leaves to an overall height of 1 ft. Paired, heart-shaped leaves are toothed and stalked, although the upper pair may be very short-stalked or sessile. These occur in cool, damp, well shaded locations presenting a delicate, fairy-like appearance. The example shown was growing in just such a spot along Green Gardens Trail, Gros Morne National Park, in Late-July.

21. DOGWOOD FAMILY
(Cornaceae)

A family with members ranging from low herbaceous plants (Bunchberry) to small trees (Flowering Dogwood). Flowers are usually small and clustered, with 4–5 petals.

1. BUNCHBERRY\CRACKER-BERRY\DWARF CORNEL
(Cornus canadensis)
A. Flower; B. Berry

A low herbaceous plant, 3–6 inches in height. Clusters of very small, greenish-white, dark-centred flowers are surrounded by 4 large white petal-like bracts. A pair of broad-oval, pointed leaves and 2 pairs of somewhat narrower, pointed leaves occur just below the flower. Leaf veins arch from the leaf base along the length of the leaf. An additional pair of smaller leaves occur at mid-stem but are not visible in the photograph. The example shown was growing in mid-July at the forest edge alongside Salmonier Line.

Fruit of *C. canadensis* is a tight cluster of shiny red single-seeded berries (drupes).The example shown was growing in early-September in approximately the same location as the flower example.

2. SWEDISH BUNCHBERRY
(Cornus suicica)

A tight cluster of small dark-purple flowers surrounded by 4 white petal-like bracts. Alternating pairs of elliptical leaves curve closely around the stem. The example shown was growing in early-July at Cape Spear.

3. RED-OSIER DOGWOOD
(Cornus stolonifera)

An erect flowering shrub to 6 ft. high with a smooth, wine-red, woody stem. Tight clusters of small white 4-petalled flowers terminate the branches. Fruit are clusters of white drupes. Leaves are opposite, broad-oval, parallel veined, dark green above and whitened on the under-surface. The example shown was growing at the west end of Long Pond, St. John's in late-June.

22. LOOSESTRIFE FAMILY
(*Lythraceae*)
Reference material indicates that there are about 25 genera and 550 species recognized within this family, most of which occur in north temperate climates. However, only one species of one genus (*Lythrum salicaria*) is recorded in Rouleau's List of Newfoundland Plants.

1. PURPLE LOOSESTRIFE
(*Lythrum salicaria*)
Dense whorls of usually 6-petalled, magenta flowers in long spikes atop 3–4 ft., sometimes branching stems. Leaves are pointed ovate, unstalked, somewhat hairy, and alternating in pairs or in threes. Flowers arise unstalked or with very short stalks from leaf axils. Petals are relatively long and slender and usually in a crumpled condition. Purple Loosestrife has a "heterostylous" flower, each plant bearing flowers having one of three possible combinations of style and stamens (A long style with medium and short stamens; a medium-length style with long and short stamens; a short style with medium and long stamens). Each type of stamen pro-

duces a different type of pollen so that fertilization occurs only between stamens and styles of the same length, avoiding self-pollination and improving the probability of cross-pollination. "Heterostyly" tends to maintain or enhance plant vitality and seems to be well proven elsewhere in Eastern Canada where the invasive vitality of *L. salicaria* into some wetland sites is notorious. However, a similar invasive trend is not apparent in Newfoundland, perhaps due to a relative lack of pollinators (flies and bees) at critical times. The example shown was growing in early-September in a small marsh near Murray's Pond beside the road from St. John's to Portugal Cove.

23. PARSLEY/CARROT FAMILY
(*Umbelliferae*)/(*Apiaceae*)
Numerous, small, 5-petalled flowers closely grouped on a single flower stalk and numerous flower stalks arising from a single point on the main stem of the flower head (umbel). Each flower has 5 stamens. Petals may vary in size. Leaves are large, alternate, and may be compound or otherwise much divided. Plant stems are usually hollow, arising from taproots or rhizomes.

1. WILD CARROT/
QUEEN ANNE'S LACE
(*Daucus carota*)
Clusters of small white, 5-petalled flowers maturing from the bud to a convex umbel; then to a flat-topped umbel presenting a lace-like pattern; eventually, when going to seed, the flower stalks of the umbel turn upward and inward forming a "cup" or "bird's nest" shape. A purple centre flower may be present during the "flat-topped" stage. The main flower stem is hairy. Leaves are finely divided and fern-like. A ring of forked, threadlike bracts occurs at the base of each umbel.

Those shown were growing in a ditch alongside the highway in early- August.

2. HEMLOCK-PARSLEY
(*Conioselinum chinense*)
Similar to *D. carota* but having less showy flowers and umbel clusters are more widely separated. Stem is smooth, more slender, and has no bracts at the base of each umbel. Finely divided, fern-like leaves with broadened stalks sheathing the stem occur mainly at the base of the plant, but a few minor or vestigal leaves occur incidentally along the upper stem. The example shown was

Signal Hill Tattoo:
Regularly throughout the summer "The Tattoo" recalls and demonstrates military activity on Signal Hill, St. John's, during the 17th and 18th centuries.

22-1

23-1

Sailing:
Sailboats leaving "The Narrows", at the annual St. John's Day race, commemorating John Cabot's "discovery" on St. John The Baptist's Day, June 24, 1497.

23-2

Baker's Brook Falls:
Reached by a comfortable 5 km walk from Berry Hill Camping Park in Gros Morne National Park.

23-3

23-3A

23-5

23-4

23-6

23-7

growing in late-August in a shady part of our front lawn and was 2-3 ft. in height. However, it is more at home in damp woodlands and along river banks where it may grow to 5 ft. or more in height.

3. COW PARSNIP
(*Heracleum maximum*)
A very large plant growing to a height of 9 ft. or more, having a thick, hollow stem with a hairy surface. Leaves are large, comprised of three coarsely toothed, maple-like leaflets, and are prominently sheathed at the junction with the stem. Umbels of white flowers are also quite large (up to 9 inches or more across), usually in groups of 3 to 4 at the upper extremity of the stem. Close inspection of an umbel reveals that flowers at the edge of each floral group have enlarged and elongated petals protruding outwards. It prefers alkaline soil and grows more profusely on the Island's west coast. The example shown was growing in mid-July beside the trail to Baker's Brook Falls in Gros Morne National Park.

3A.
Close-up picture of a flower umbel taken at Indian Head Park, Stephenville in early-July of the previous year.

4. CARAWAY
(*Carum carvi*)
Large umbels of small white flowers terminate each leafy branch alternating up a thick, hollow, hairless stem. Leaves are finely disected, feathery, whorled around the leaf-stalk, and prominently sheathed at stem juncture. Forked bracts occur at growth-nodes of the upper stem. The example shown was growing at Watt's Point Calcareous Barrens in mid-July. Its occurance there seems somewhat at odds with its being considered an introduced species. Nevertheless, it must be remembered that the relic of a coastal roadway through this area was at one time, not so long ago, the highway route connecting St. Anthony and other settlements at the tip of the Great Northern Peninsula with the rest of the Island to the south; and prior to introduction of the automobile it was a well used cart track.

5. SCOTCH LOVAGE
(*Ligusticum scothicum*)
A clumping, bushy plant up to 2 ft. high with broad, white umbels terminating its smooth dark-purple stems; sparsely leafed in upper portions. Leaves are pinnate with 3 pointed oval terminal leaflets toothed along the outer margin. The example shown was growing in isolation from other growth on Tors Cove Beach in mid-August, not far from a fish processing plant.

6. ANGELICA/ALEXANDERS/ EMBLOCH
(*Angelica atropurpurea*)
Tightly crowded umbels of small white flowers atop smooth, stout, wine-red stems 3 ft. or more in height. Leaves are pinnate with pointed-oval to lance-shaped leaflets similar to *L. scothicum*, but shiny and not so densely growing. The example shown was growing in abundance along the shoreline of Daniel's Point, Trepassey in early-August.

7. WOODLAND CHERVIL
(*Anthriscus sylvestris*)
Umbels of white flowers atop smooth, green stems up to 5 ft. or more in height. Prefers moist soil conditions along river banks where it forms fairly extensive colonies. Its leaves are soft and fern-like, the large lower leaves tri-pinnate and smaller upper leaves bi-pinnate. The example shown was photographed in June at Bowring Park.

Bowring Park, located on the Waterford River flowing from Mount Pearl and discharging into St. John's Harbour, was developed by the historically and commercially prominent merchant firm of Bowring

Brothers Limited and turned over to the City of St. John's in 1914. In more recent times adjoining land, once the property of Sir Richard Squires (Prime Minister 1919-23 and 1928-32 during the period of Responsible Government), has been added to the Park. The entire length of the river's floodplain is now designated for environmental protection and development as a walking trail system. The now-vacated CN Railway Route running parallel with the river will also soon be integrated with this extensive linear open space. Eventually this may result in regeneration of the natural beauty once associated with the Waterford River system.

8. WILD PARSNIP
(Pastinica sativa)

Umbels of small yellow flowers at the extremity of smooth branches growing from a stout, furrowed stem. Leaves are bright green, pinnate with relatively broad, coarsely toothed leaflets. The example shown was growing in our backyard in late summer, where I had planted parsnip many years before but had done an incomplete job of harvesting. The lance-leafed bush in the background is pin-cherry (Prunus pensylvanica), a member of the rose family.

24. GINSING FAMILY
(Araliaceae)

Flowering members of this family resemble the Parsley/Carrot family, having small flowers of similar form and pinnate leaves. However, where flowers are in umbels, the umbel is usually of a rounder form. Fruit is a berry rather than a dry seed-case. Genera of this family include ivy (Hedera), ginsing (Panax), and sarsparilla (Aralia). Of these, only two species of Aralia (A. hispida and A. nudicaulis) are noted in Rouleau's List as being found in Newfoundland. A third species, A. racemosa (spikenard) is recorded as being present in Atlantic Canada.

1. BRISTLY SARSPARILLA
(Aralia hispida)

This species has a bristled stem, at least at its base, and may grow to a height of 3 ft. Long bi-pinnate leaves divide into two or three leaf-fronds at or near the stem, each frond bearing 3–7 oblong to oval, pointed, sharp-toothed leaflets. Flower umbels occur either as long-stalked clusters on the upper stem or arise from leaf axils. The example shown was growing atop Mt. Scio, St. John's in Mid-August. Stems are reddish-purple and appear to be smooth rather than bristly.

2. WILD SARSPARILLA
(Aralia nudicaulis)

Smooth-stemmed and smaller than A. hispida, its flower and single leaf stalk arise separately from the ground. Its 3-part leaf is taller than the flower and has more finely toothed leaflets than A. hispida. The example shown was growing at Shallow Bay Camping Park, Gros Morne National Park in mid-July.

2A.

A specimen of Aralia showing characteristics of A. hispida, having 7 leaflets per leaf division; some leaves arising from the flower stem; and the flower stem rises well above the leaves. However, it also has characteristics of A. nudicaulis having a smooth, and in one instance leafless, stem. A complicating factor is that flower umbels arise variously along the stem. This specimen was growing in mid-August near Seal Cove River, Seal Cove, Conception Bay.

Trepassey:
Old cannons which once protected the area from french invasion by sea, on a prominence over-looking Trepassey, a fishing community at the southern extremity of the Avalon Peninsula.

Bowring Park:
"The Duck Pond" (once "The Boat Pond") at Bowring Park east entry, St. John's.

23-8

24-1   24-2   24-2A

25-1

25-2

Point Riche Lighthouse:
*Overlooking the Gulf of St. Lawrence. Burial sites and
other artifacts of The Red Ochre People who inhabited
this area 5,000 years ago were unearthed in this vicinity
and are displayed nearby in an archeological museum
at Port Aux Choix.*

25-3

25-4

25-5

25. WINTERGREEN FAMILY
(Pyrolaceae)

Small, nodding, 5-petalled, woodland plants usually in a loose raceme on a slender, leafless, unbranched stem rising from a basal rosette of round to oval, stalked leaves. A prominently projecting style is a characteristic feature. The genera of this family are sometimes included in the Heath Family (*Ericaceae*). On the other hand, genera which are more clearly saprophytic, such as *Monotropa*, are sometimes assigned to a separate family (*Monotropaceae*). These latter are included here in the Wintergreen Family.

1. ONE-FLOWERED WINTERGREEN
(*Moneses uniflora*)

A single, nodding, waxy white, 5-petalled, star-shaped flower with a prominently displayed ovary from which projects a straight, stiff style ending in a 4-pronged stigma. Paired, knobby-ended stamen project below the ovary along each petal. The flower nods on its leafless stem when in bloom, but straightens upright when in fruit. Note the single, scale-like, green to whitish bract on the upper stem. Stalked basal evergreen leaves are round to oval and slightly toothed. The example shown was growing beneath coniferous trees at Catamaran Camping Park in early-July.

2. PINK PYROLA
(*Pyrola asarifolia*)

A raceme of pink to deep red, nodding, 5-petalled flowers with a long, curved, pink style projecting beyond the petals. Its straight, deep red stem rises from a basal rosette of finely-toothed, heart-shaped leaves (not seen in picture). A single red scale-like bract occurs below the raceme. The example shown was growing in mid-July at Point Riche on the Great Northern Peninsula. The Wintergreen Family is said to be dependent on mycorrhizal fungi associated with conifers. However these and many others were growing in open, sunlit, grassland and in other low ground cover locations. In these cases it may well be that either common or trailing juniper are the "conifers" enabling mycorrhizal association.

3. WHITE WINTERGREEN/ SHINLEAF
(*Pyrola elliptica*)

A raceme of white-petalled, broadly cupped, nodding flowers having long, green, curving styles extending beyond the petals. The straight, smooth stem bears 1 or 2 small bracts below the flower raceme. The example shown was growing in mid-August in a marsh near Seal Cove River, upstream from the Conception Bay Highway. Note the withered basal leaves barely projecting above the moss. We have also found these growing in mid-July at the foot of The Tablelands in Gros Morn National Park, a drier location, but also with withered basal leaves. The specimens there had 10–12 flowers per raceme, but the photograph did not show the long styles so clearly.

4. LESSER PYROLA
(*Pyrola minor*)

A raceme of white to pale pink, nodding, 5-petalled flowers; smaller and with petals more cupped than in *P. asarifolia*. The style is also shorter and does not project beyond the petals. Leaves, also in a basal rosette typical of the family, are hidden by the low ground cover of strawberry and crackerberry leaves. The example shown was growing in early-July at Catamaran Camping Park at the same time as *M. uniflora*.

5. ONE-SIDED WINTERGREEN
(*Pyrola secunda*)

Racemes of small greenish-white globular flowers hanging from one side of a smooth pinkish stem. Small bracts occur along the stem at the base of flower stalks. Note that the style is long enough for the 4-pronged stigma to project beyond the petals. The example shown was growing in mid-July near Bay Bulls. This flower may sometimes be noted as a separate genus – *Orthilia*.

6. INDIAN PIPE/CORPSE PLANT/GHOST FLOWER
(*Monotropa uniflora*)
A single, waxy-white, nodding flower having 5 overlapping petals and 5 similarly white sepals forming a bell shape. Usually found growing up to 10 inches high in groups or clumps from organic groundcover of mature coniferous forests. The fleshy stem is also waxy-white as are the vestigal leaves, here reduced to scale-like bracts alternating along the stem. A larger bract forms a hood over the nodding flower. A brown seed capsule is formed on maturity and the capsule then assumes an upright position. The example shown was growing in late-August at Power's Pond off Thorburn Road, just beyond the St. John's Windsor Lake water supply catchment area boundary.

26. DIAPENSIA FAMILY
(*Diapensiaceae*)
A small family of 5-part, single-stemmed flowers with evergreen leaves, sometimes included with the Heath Family. *Diapensia lapponica* is the only member of this family included in Rouleau's List Of Newfoundland Plants.

1. GROUND IVORY / MOSS LILY
(*Diapensia lapponica*)
Small, white, bell-shaped, 5-lobed flowers occurring singly on short stalks arising from whorls of small, oval, untoothed, evergreen, mat-forming leaves. In the example shown, each flower appears to be supported by a ring of 5 sepal-like bracts which overlap the 5 sepals, all of which persist to form the seed capsule. Petal lobes are reflexed, allowing the 5 paired stamens and the central pistil to project out of the petal tube. These were growing in mid-August on the exposed meadowland atop the cliffs near the Bird Sanctuary at Cape St. Mary's.

27. HEATH FAMILY
(*Ericaceae*)
Low woody shrubs or trailing plants, usually occurring on acid soils in temperate and northern regions. Flowers have a single central pistil cupped by 4–5 usually fused petals with 1 or 2 stamens per petal.

1. LABRADOR TEA
(*Ledum groenlandicum*)
A dense, terminal cluster of white, 5-petalled flowers. Stamens protrude conspicuously giving the flower head a fuzzy appearance. Leaves are evergreen, leathery, narrowly elliptical, untoothed, rolled under at the edges and have a brown woolly undersurface. This plant does not usually exceed 3 ft. in height. The example shown was growing in early-June near the CBC Building on Prince Philip Parkway, St. John's.

2. SHEEP LAUREL/LAMBKILL
(*Kalmia angustifolia*)
A lateral cluster of bright pink, dish-shaped flowers emerging below the leafy apex of the plant. Each flower is comprised of 5 joined petals, 10 radiating stamens secured to the bottom of the flower dish until disturbed by

25-6

26-1

27-2

27-1

Cape St. Mary's: *(Below, left)*
Gannets cover a 200 ft. cliff.

Fall Colours: *(Below)*
Colours peak in mid-October

27-3A

27-3

27-4

27-5

27-6

27-7

27-7A

a foraging insect, and a protruding pistil. Leaves are evergreen, paired or in whorls of 3, glossy, larger than Labrador Tea (*L. groenlandicum*), not rolled at the edges and do not have a woolly undersurface. The example shown was also growing near the CBC Building on Prince Philip Parkway, St. John's, in the same general location as Labrador Tea, but in late-June.

3. PALE LAUREL/BOG LAUREL
(*Kalmia polifolia*)
This has the same pink, dish-shaped flower as sheep laurel (*K. angustifolia*), but occurs in smaller and terminal clusters on lower-growing woody stems (the one shown being not more than 6 inches high). Leaves are sparser, very narrowly elliptical (almost needle-like), rolled under at the edge, and have a whitened undersurface. The example shown was growing in early-July on a peat barrens alongside the Burin Peninsula Highway. Note the extensive lichen cover (*Cladonia alpestris*).

3A.
A white form of Kalmia polifolia (*Var. leucantha*) growing at Watt's Point Calcareous Barrens in mid-July.

4. RHODORA
(*Rhododendron canadense*)

Said one bee to the others,
in its wibbly-wobbly way:
"You should see what I saw
near the brook down by the bay.
The woods are full of pinky-purple
and the scent is so divine!
What's more, you get a tummy-rub
where e'er you go to dine."

Clusters of magenta, 5-petalled flowers appearing along with new leaves at the tip of twiggy stems. The 3 upper petals are fused for about half their length forming a 3-lobed upper lip. Flowers face to the side (lateral facing) and have 10 long upward-curving stamens and a similarly upward-curving but somewhat longer pistil. Leaves are narrow-

ly elliptical, untoothed, and rolled under at the edge. Those shown were growing at Aspen Brook Picnic Park, a little way west of Grand Falls, in mid-June.

5. HEATHER/LING
(*Calluna vulgaris*)
The only place we have found this growing in the wild is at Whitbourne, where it forms an extensive ground cover alongside the old railway track and along the roadside near the railway crossing. Being so localized, it is presumed to have been introduced to the area by Sir Robert Bond and has since prospered and naturalized to a point where it has become a feature of natural beauty which should be protected and preserved.

6. SMALL CRANBERRY/ MARSHBERRY
(*Vaccinium oxycoccus*)
A small, fine-stemmed, creeping shrub, commonly found in peaty marshlands. Flowers are nodding and occur singly at the extremity of paired 2-inch, ascending stalks having two small bracts about half way up. The flower's 4 pink petals are fully recurved and the pistil and stamens project snout-like downward. Leaves are evergreen, small, oval or elliptical, alternate, and well separated along the stem. The example shown was growing in mid-July on a bog near Stephenville.

7. PARTRIDGEBERRY/MOUNTAIN CRANBERRY
(*Vaccinium vitis-idaea*)
A low creeping evergreen shrub bearing 3 or more 4-petalled, white to pink, bell-shaped, nodding flowers in terminal clusters. Leaves are shiny and may vary in colour from bright green to a dark reddish green, and in shape from oval to elliptical. Those shown were growing at Indian Arm Pond in mid-July.

7A.
Berries are a deep red to wine colour, soft, juicy and tart tasting when ripe. Picking sea-

son follows or overlaps the end of the blue-berry season. The picking season for these usually starts in mid-September.

8. BLUEBERRY/WHORTS (HURTS) (*Vaccinium angustifolium*)

A low, woody shrub bearing clusters or racemes of white, pink-tinged, urn-shaped flowers. The urn shape is formed by the fusion of 5 petals, recognized by the 5 short lobes which form a fluting around the urn opening to the pistil and stamens. The example shown was growing in early-July along-side the Burin Peninsula Highway.

8A.

The fruit is a blue berry widely picked in late August and early September for family use. It is also a source of considerable commercial revenue as a resource industry. Blueberry plants are highly variable in that they hybridize easily among the several varieties that occur in the Province and characteristics vary with different soil and environmental conditions. The example shown was growing in late-September beside Higgins Line, near Confederation Building, St. John's.

9. DWARF HUCKLEBERRY (*Gaylussacia dumosa*)

A low twiggy shrub bearing one-sided racemes of white to pink, 5-lobed, vase-shaped flowers. The petal lobes are pointed and the tips reflexed. The 5 fused sepals at the base of the flower are sharply pointed and edged with a bright red colour. Leaves are oval to elliptical but wedge-shaped at the base. Leaf edges are fringed with small hairs and there is a noticeable extension of the mid-vein forming a small tip at the end of the leaf. The example shown was growing in mid-August on a marsh near the upper course of Seal Cove River, Conception Bay.

10. CRYSTAL-BERRY/BOG ROSEMARY (*Andromeda glaucophylla*)

Throughout the marsh hang treasure-drops,
by morning sunlight kissed.
Arrayed in sparkling splendour
by the early morning mist.
Who venture to disturb these jewels,
beneath a dragon's mane,
And gaze into the crystal pink,
are ne'er the same again.

Delicate, pink, urn-shaped flowers in nod-ding clusters at the extremity of low twiggy stalks growing in peaty marshland. The colour shades from pink at the 5 petal-tips at the mouth of the urn, to a white base, white sepals and flower stalk. Leaves are ever-green, erect, needle-like (as a result of severely rolled edges) and are whitened underneath. The example shown was pho-tographed in early-July on a marsh beside the Burin Peninsula Highway.

11. LEATHERLEAF (*Chamaedaphne calyculata*)

White, urn-shaped, drooping flowers in one-sided racemes at the extremity of woody, evergreen shrubs growing to a height of 3 feet or more in wet habitats. Note also the creamy-white sepals at the base of the flower. Leaves are oval to elliptical, dull green on the upper surface, a lighter or olive green beneath, and are minutely toothed. The example shown was growing at Oxen Pond Botanic Park in mid-June. The name "gold-withy" or "gould-withy" is also commonly applied to this and a variety of other bushy plants found in barrens and marshes. I remember well using the term "gooly bushes" in my younger years, and use the term on occasion even now.

27-8

27-8A

27-9

27-10

Spider's Web:
Beads of dew along the strands reveal its
pattern and precise construction.

27-11

27-12

27-13

27-14

Triangle, Coastal Labrador:
View from deck of the coastal boat "Northern Ranger". Many small communities along the Labrador coast are in snug inlets which cannot be safely entered by coastal freighter. Goods, people and baggage must therefore be transferred offshore.

28-1

28-1A

12. ALPINE AZALIA
(*Loisleuria procumbens*)

Small, pink, 5-petalled, bell-shaped flowers opening upwards in few-flowered, short-stalked, terminal clusters on much-branched, twiggy stems forming a tussock. Leaves are evergreen, leathery, short, rounded at the tip and sufficiently dense to present a matted appearance. These were growing at Watt's Point Calcareous Barrens in early- to mid-June. Note also the variety of other growth protruding through the tussock and peripheral to it, particularly Pink Crowberry (*Empetrum eamesii*), indicating an interdependence for survival commonly apparent throughout the Calcareous Barrens, but much less noticeable elsewhere.

13. TRAILING ARBUTUS
(*Epigaea repens*)

A prostrate, evergreen shrub having terminal clusters of waxy 5-petalled, tube-shaped flowers, shading from pink at the petal tips to white at the base of the flower tube. Leaves are large, oval, leathery and with a hairy leaf-stalk. Branch stems are green to greenish-brown and covered with brown hairs. It occurs naturally on the West Coast of the Island, but the example shown was growing in the Botanic Park on Mt. Scio Road, St. John's in mid-June.

14. ARCTIC WHITE HEATHER
(*Cassiope tetragona*)

Solitary, white, nodding, bell-shaped flowers with yellow-green sepals on erect, smooth, yellow-green stems. They arise at or near the up-turned leafy ends of usually prostrate woody branches. Short, stubby, elliptical leaves occur in dense, overlapping whorls and curve upwards, spoon-like, around the central nerve, thus appearing more like stubby needles. The flower turns upwards when in fruit. When the photograph was taken the capsule had opened to release the matured seed. The green-pigmented chlorophyll is no longer present, thus making the remaining yellow pigment the dominent colour. The example shown was growing in early-September at Cape Charles, Labrador.

28. CROWBERRY FAMILY
(*Empetraceae*)

Very low, mat-forming, woody shrubs with narrow, needle-like, evergreen leaves. Tiny, pinkish, 3-part flowers (3 petals, 3 sepals, 3 stamens) occur in leaf axils on the outerbranches. Three species occur in the Province: Black Crowberry (*Empetrum nigrum*), whose fruit is a dull black berry (drupe); Pink Crowberry (*Empetrum eamesii*), bearing a shiny red berry; and Purple Crowberry (*Empetrum atropurpurium*), bearing a dark-red to plum-coloured berry. Black Crowberry is the commonest and Purple Crowberry the least common. Indications are that these low shrubs are long-lasting but very slow-growing, to an extent that even a small mat or clump may represent 50 years or more of growth. Crowberry has characteristics very similar to Heath and is sometimes included as a member of the Heath Family.

1. PINK CROWBERRY
(*Empetrum eamesii*)

Flowers may be hermaphrodite or dioecious. Leaves are narrow-oval with strongly in-rolled edges, giving them a needle-like appearance. Stems and branches are twiggy with leaves usually bunched at the outer extremities. Young branches are densely cov-ered with white hairs. The example shows Pink Crowberry fruit growing in late-August atop the Hawk Hills, about 5 miles inland from Holyrood, Conception Bay, at an elevation of 600–700 feet.

A. BLACK CROWBERRY
(*Empetrum nigrum*)

29. PRIMROSE FAMILY
(*Primulaceae*)

Most members of the family are radially symmetrical and have 5 petals, 5 sepals, 5 stamens and a single style. In some the petals open fully and in others the petals may be fused at the base forming a short tube. Stamens occur at the centre of the petal base rather than between petals as is the case with most other 5-petalled flowers. Typically, flowers are in terminal umbels with a rosette of leaves at the base of the stem. However, flowers may also be in spikes or arise singly from leaf axils along a leafy stem. Some species of the family exhibit a characteristic whereby one plant of the species may have a long style and short stamens, while a neighbouring plant of the same species may have a short style and long stamens (heterostylous); thus increasing the probability of cross-fertilization and decreasing the probability of self-fertilization.

1. BIRD'S-EYE PRIMROSE
(*Primula laurentiana*)

Pink, mauve or white 5-petalled flowers with a yellow centre in an umbel at the top of a leafless, sometimes powdery-whitened stem. Petals conspicuously notched on the outer edge. Oval, paddle-shaped leaves, slightly toothed along the outer edge, form a rosette at the base of the stem. The example shown was growing in mid-July at "The Arches", a scenic park just north of Gros Morne National Park. Note that the fused, whitened and ridged sepals extend upwards encasing the tube portion of the petals for its entire length. Another variation is shown as follows:

1A.

A very small specimen, no more than 3 inches high, growing at Watt's Point Calcareous Barrens in early-June. Note the relatively broad leaf base, pointed leaf tips, and absence of marginal teeth. A pair of sessile leaves also occurs part way up the flower stem.

2. GREENLAND PRIMROSE
(*Primula egaliksensis*)

A white-flowered, non-powdery species growing in mid-July at Eddies Cove where the highway turns inland towards St. Anthony on the Great Northern Peninsula. Note the numerous stems rising from the clustered rosette of spatulate, untoothed basal leaves;

the fleshy bracts at the base of the flower umbels; the very short flower stalks; and that the sepals extend only part way up the tube formed by the fused petals.

3. STARFLOWER
(*Trientalis borealis*)

The 6–7 white, pointed petals give the flower its name. The number of stamens is equal to the number of petals. There may be 1–3 flowers rising on threadlike stalks from the centre of a whorl of 5–10 shiny, lance-shaped, pointed, untoothed leaves atop an otherwise bare 4–6 inch stalk. Overall, the flower is 4–8 inches tall and blooms in early Spring at the same time as Canada Mayflower (*Maianthemum canadense*). Together they give a fairy-like quality to the forest floor. The example shown has but one 7-petalled flower and 7 leaves. Note the network of fine veins in the leaf and the vein paralleling the leaf edge. A wasp is approaching one of the neighbouring mayflowers. The example shown was growing among the trees at the head of Long Pond on MUN Campus in early-June.

4. YELLOW LOOSESTRIFE/ SWAMP CANDLES
(*Lysimachia terrestris*)

Yellow, star-shaped, 5-part flowers in a many-flowered terminal raceme atop a single, unbranched, sturdy and leafy stem up to 3 feet tall. Leaves are paired, short-stalked

29-1A

29-1

The Arches:
*A picnic park on the Viking Trail, north of Gros Morne
National park, featuring the eroded remnants of an earlier
shoreline.*

29-2

29-3

29-4

29-5

Horses:
Now seldom used as work animals, these were grazing
in Point au Mal Picnic Park; a quiet, scenic park well
away from commonly traveled routes.

29-6

29-7

30-1A

30-1B

to sessile, and pointed lanceolate, sometimes quite narrowly so. A pair of red spots at the base of each petal is sometimes quite noticeable. The example shown was growing in a marsh near Southwest Pond on the Salmonier Line in mid-August.

5. WHORLED LOOSESTRIFE
(*Lysimachia quadrifolia*)
Flowers arise from axils of long-stalked upper leaves, instead of long terminal racemes as in Swamp Candles (*Lysimachia terrestris*). Leaves in stalked whorls of 3 or 4. Hybrids of this with *L. terrestris*, although sterile, are capable of spreading vegetatively. The example shown was growing at Jack's Pond Camping Park in late-August.

6. GARDEN LOOSESTRIFE
(*Lysimachia punctata*)
Coarse, hairy, pointed-ovate leaves in whorls of 4 on tall, hairy stems up to 4 ft. or more in height. Flowers have broad, overlapping, yellow petals and arise in stalked whorls

from the axils of the upper leaves. The example shown was growing in a section of Bowring Park preserved over the years as a naturalized area. It is found also as a garden escape in many places throughout the Island portion of the Province.

7. SEA MILKWORT
(*Glaux maritima*)
A coastal species found in shallow water and marshes bordering saltwater ponds and tidal estuaries. The flower has no petals, but the 5 round-lobed, white to pink sepals look like petals and form a bell-shape around the 5 yellow-tipped stamens and pistil. The stalkless flowers occur singly in leaf axils of the paired, oval, fleshy, sessile leaves. The stem is smooth, sturdy, fleshy, usually light-green and up to 6 inches in height. The example shown was growing in a shallow tidal pond at the back of a beach at Point au Mal Picnic Park, a few miles north along the unpaved coastal road from the narrow isthmus of the Port au Port Peninsula.

30. LEADWORT/SEA-LAVENDER FAMILY
(*Plumbaginaceae*)
Plants associated mainly with maritime locations. Flowers are 5-parted with fused, usually papery-textured sepals, occurring either in one-sided, usually branching, racemes (corymbs) as in the Sea-Lavender genus *Limonium*; or in tight terminal clusters as in the genus *Armeria*. Leaves are usually in a basal rosette, either linear and grass-like or spatulate. Only 1 of each genus (*L. carolinianum* and *A. maritima*) is recorded in Rouleau's List as occurring in Newfoundland. The former is considered a doubtful entry and we have not come across it in our travels.

1. THRIFT
(*Armeria maritima*)
Usually called Thrift but may locally be called Straw-flower or Fox-flower, it has a single tight terminal cluster of small purplish-pink, 5-lobed, bell-like petals with papery sepals. A ring of bracts underlies the flower head and sheaths the uppermost portion of the 6–12 inch, smooth, leafless, unbranched stem. Basal leaves are short, linear and grass-like. It is commonly found as tufts increasing in size over time by means of woody, branching rootstock. Numerous flowered stems rise well

above the mat or tuft of leaves. Two examples are shown.

1A.
A tuft of flowers growing in early-June at Watt's Point Calcareous Barrens.

1B.
A closer view of matured flower heads growing in the same area in mid-July. Long stems of one of the Rush Family (*Juncaceae*) are also seen in the photograph and may easily be mistaken as leaves of *A. Maritima*.

31. DOGBANE FAMILY
(*Apocynaceae*)

Most members of this family are shrubs and vines of warmer climates, many having poisonous sap, examples of these being Oleander, Frangipani, and Indian Hemp. Flowers are 5-petalled with sepals and petals fused and lobed.

1. SPREADING DOGBANE
(*Apocynum androsaemifolium*)

A leafy shrub up to 4 ft. tall with smooth, usually reddish stems. Its flowers are fragrant, pink, bell-like with recurved petal lobes, and dangle in stalked clusters from leaf axils of paired, opposite, ovate, straight-edged, short-stalked or sessile leaves. Note the pink stripes inside the flower bell. The example shown was growing in late-July in the floodplain of Seal Cove River, Conception Bay. We have also found it, flowering at the same time, at Indian Arm Pond, west of Gander in Central Newfoundland.

2. PERIWINKLE/MYRTLE
(*Vinca minor*)

A low-growing, creeping plant with purplish-blue flowers, often used as ground cover in gardens and cemeteries and is commonly found as an "escape" in and around many of these locations. The flower petals are fused only near their base from which they spread separately outward. Curved sides and straight outside edges present a pinwheel effect. The example shown was growing in mid-June as shaded ground cover at Bowring Park, St. John's.

32. GENTIAN FAMILY
(*Gentianaceae*)

Flower parts (petals, stamens, sepals) are axially symmetrical, usually in 5's but may vary among species from 4–12. The lower portion of sepals and petals are often fused forming a tube. Leaves are paired, linearly veined, untoothed, usually sessile, and pointed-elliptical in shape. Flowers arise from upper leaf axils either singly or in stalked or stalkless clusters.

1. NORTHERN GENTIAN/ AUTUMN GENTIAN
(*Gentianella amarella*)

Tubular, purple-petalled flowers arising on short flower-stalks from the axils of paired, sessile, triangular-shaped leaves. The stem is angular in cross-section and both stem and leaves are purple-tinged. The example shown was growing in mid-September in damp sandy soil at Forteau on the southern coast of Labrador. The plant shown is strongly branched at the base and the branches are sharply ascendant giving it an overall spire-like appearance. There were many of these scattered thinly throughout the area, all with the same basal branching. This is not a descriptive feature included in our reference material. It may be a local variety, the result of inbreeding (cleistogamy) necessitated by the absence of pollinating insects at the time of maturity, due to the onset of colder temperatures in the latter part of August on the south coast of Labrador. It is also noted that some taxonomists include this species in the genus *Gentiana*, while others recognize a separate genus *Gentianella*.

Seal Cove, Conception Bay:
*A backwater pond in the floodplain of Seal Cove River,
downstream from the Conception Bay Highway.*

31-1

Pinware River, Labrador:
*A noted salmon river in south coastal
Labrador, the Pinware is crossed by a bridge
on the 50 miles of paved road from L'Anse
au Claire to Red Bay.*

31-2

32-1

32-2

32-3

Flat Bay:
A shallow southern arm of St. Georges Bay. Here a narrow neck of land extends out from the community of Flat Bay.

32-4   32-5   33-

2. ISLAND GENETIAN
(*Genetiana nesophila*)

Single, relatively large, 4-part flowers having 4 overlapping, blue-violet, slightly fringed, recurved petals, cupped by 4 yellow-green, pointed sepals. Its smooth, square, leafless stem is dark-red, unbranched, and is usually shorter than the flower. Leaves are basal, elliptical, sessile to clasping, untoothed and curve upwards around the central nerve. The example shown was growing at Point Riche in mid-July.

3. SPURRED GENTIAN
(*Halenia deflexa*)

Clusters of 2–5 stalkless or very short-stalked, urn-shaped, cream petalled flowers, with reddish-purple petal-like sepals, occur terminally and in leaf axils. Petals are fused, forming the urn shape, and are lobed, the lobes barely extending beyond the sepals. Each sepal has a pair of spurs extending backwards, terminating in a dark-purple knob. A smaller but similarly coloured bract curves upwards between the spurs. The stem is 6–8 inches high, square in cross-section, smooth and pale green. Leaves are paired, pointed-oval, sessile, 3–5 veined, and are untoothed. The example shown was growing on a marshy hillside near Flatbay, on the west coast of the Island, south of Stephenville, in mid-July, and was keeping close company with a group of Yellow Rattle (*Rhinanthus spp.*).

4. MARSH FELWORT/ STAR GENTIAN
(*Lomatogonium rotatum*)

A 5-parted, fully opening gentian having pointed white petals suffused with blue. The flowers and buds are relatively large for this 3-6 inch plant and arise singly on stalks from leaf axils. Leaves are paired, ovate from multiple squarely angled, purplish stems. The example shown was growing in late-August in open grassy areas near a cemetery at St. Anthony. Note that, when open, the sepals extend beyond the petals.

5. BOGBEAN/BUCKBEAN
(*Menyanthes trifoliata*)

A terminal raceme of mainly 5-part flowers with white, densely bearded petals fused at the base, but with widely reflexed tips and a prominent pistil, – rather lily-like. Leaves are on separate stems having 3 oval, sometimes slightly toothed, pinnately veined leaflets. It is an aquatic plant of shallow-water or marshy locations, its leaves and flowers rising just above the surface of the water. The example shown was growing in late-May at the west end of Long Pond, St. John's. Note that one of the flowers has 6 petals and 6 pairs of stamens rather than the usual 5, indicating a variability of these characteristics. [Buckbean, together with Floating Hearts (*Nymphoides spp.*), is sometimes placed in a small separate family – Menyanthaceae.]

33. MORNING GLORY FAMILY
(*Convolvulaceae*)

Most plants in this family are climbers with twining stems. Flowers have 5-parted sepals, petals and stamens. Petals are commonly fused forming a trumpet shape. Rouleau's List of Newfoundland Plants records only one species, *C. sepium*.

1. HEDGE BINDWEED
(*Calystegia/Convolvulus sepium*)

Some sources refer to the genus *Calystegia*, others to *Convolvulus*. In either case the species *C. sepium* is a counter-clockwise twining vine, climbing to a height of 5–6 ft. The flower is usually pure white, its petals fused into a trumpet shape, the outer margin reflexed when fully open. Flowers arise singly from leaf axils on long curving stems.

Each flower blooms and wilts in a 24-hour period. Leaves are alternate and arrow-shaped with blunt lobes. The example shown was growing alongside the old highway route on Topsail Hill in early-September.

34. BEDSTRAW/MADDER FAMILY
(*Rubiaceae*)

A fairly large, mainly tropical, family which includes gardenia, coffee and quinine plants. Most occurrences in our area are those of the *Galium* genus (Bedstraws). Clusters of tiny 4-petalled flowers with sepals and petals fused forming a tube terminating in 4 spreading petal lobes. The stem is usually slender, square and rough with whorls of narrow pointed leaves.

1. MARSH BEDSTRAW
(*Galium palustre*)

Numerous small white 4-part flowers on branching stems. Short, narrow-elliptical, untoothed leaves in whorls of 4 at branch junctures (may be paired on the upper stem). Stems are erect, relatively long and thin, often found as a tangled mass. The example shown was growing in mid-July at Bay Bulls, a small fishing community south of St. John's. This bay opens to the southeast and is usually ice-free when, occasionally in early spring, northeasterly winds blow the ice floe hard up against the land, sometimes closing the Port of St. John's to marine traffic.

2. LABRADOR BEDSTRAW
(*Galium labradoricum*)

Tiny white 4-part flowers usually in small terminal groups of 3. Stem is branched, the main stem noticeably angled (square in cross-section) and tinged reddish. Leaves are elliptical or spatulate, sessile or very short-stalked, and usually in whorls of 4. The example shown was growing in mid-August near the shoreline of Fitzgerald's Pond, a camping park on the highway to Argentia, the site of a seasonal ferry link to North Sydney, Nova Scotia during the tourist sea-

son. Argentia is also the site of a United States naval and air force military base developed during World War II, and recently transferred back to Provincial ownership.

3. WILD MADDER
(*Galium mollugo*)

A comparatively stout-stemmed plant with numerous, many-flowered spikes of small white 4-part flowers arising from leaf axils of the upper stem. Stamens project noticeably from the flower. Whorls of 6–8 narrow leaves occur at regular intervals up the smooth stem. The stems may be erect or reclining, but are usually found in tangled masses. The example shown was growing in late-July beside Leary's Brook, along Prince Philip Parkway, St. John's.

4. ROUGH BEDSTRAW
(*Galium asprellum*)

Similar to Wild Madder but has fine, recurved prickles along the stem which catch in clothing and can be felt with fingers, but are otherwise not readily apparent. Also, stamens have much shorter filaments and do not project so noticeably. The example shown was growing in late-August at Jack's Pond Camping Park.

44

34-1

34-2

Spring Ice:
A tongue of ice creeps into St. John's Bay from the main
ice pack extending to the horizon beyond Cape Spear, the
most easterly point of Newfoundland.

34-3

Autumn Gold:
A picnic site in Pippy Park, St. John's, glows in reflected
sunlight.

34-4

35-1

36-1

Placentia:
Town of Placentia, viewed from Castle Hill in summer of 1962. It was the centre of France's operations in Newfoundland from 1600 to 1713. Castle Hill was established as a National Historic Park in 1968.

36-2

36-3

36-4

35. PHLOX FAMILY
(Polemoniaceae)

No member of this family is known to be native to the province and none are referenced in Rouleau's List of Newfoundland Plants. However, Jacob's Ladder (*Polemonium spp.*) and Garden Phlox (*Phlox paniculata*) have been cultivated in Newfoundland gardens, the latter so abundantly successful that garden escapes are relatively common to an extent that it is deemed useful to include this species here.

1. GARDEN PHLOX
(*Phlox paniculata*)

Branching clusters of pink 5-petalled flowers atop 2–3 ft. upright stems. Leaves are paired, sessile or short-stalked, untoothed and lance-shaped to broadly pointed-ovate. Flower petals are fused at the base forming a long narrow tube in which a 3-pronged style and 5 stamens are contained. Petal lips flare outwards at the extremity of the tube forming the conspicuous portion of the flower. The example shown was growing at Murray's Pond, Portugal Cove in mid-September.

36. FORGET-ME-NOT FAMILY
(*Boraginaceae*)

Symmetrical flowers consisting of 5 petals, sepals and stamens and a single, central style. Leaves are usually alternate and undivided. Flowers commonly occur initially on a one-sided coiled raceme (cyme), uncoiling with maturity.

1. SEA-LUNGWORT/OYSTERLEAF
(*Mertensia maritima*)

A prostrate, fleshy, radiating, coastal plant with rose to blue-coloured, bell-shaped flowers projecting from leaf axils. Broad, pointed-oval, gray-green, alternate, fleshy leaves clasp the purplish stem. Both stem and leaves are covered with a whitish coating, giving the plant an overall misty-green appearance. The example shown was growing on a beach at Gooseberry Cove, Placentia Bay, on the road to Cape St. Mary's in early-July. "Blue Bonnet" and "Ice Plant" are local names sometimes applied to this plant. Leaves and buds of Sea Rocket (*Cakile edentula*) are also seen to the right of the photograph.

2. COMMON COMFREY
(*Symphytum officinale*)

Creamy-white, bell-shaped flowers alternate along paired racemes arising from thick stems which tend to become recumbent as this rather massive plant matures. Leaves are large, lance-shaped, untoothed but crinkled along the edge and deeply net-veined. The base of the leaves curve into and run along the stem making the stem appear to be winged. Lower leaves may be broad-oval with a winged leaf-stalk. The example shown was growing in mid-September beside Rennie's River Walking Trail, St. John's.

3. SMALL BUGLOSS
(*Lycopsis arvensis*)

Tiny mauve to white flowers projecting from leaf axils at the extremity of relatively thick, purplish, very hairy, radiating stems. Leaves are long-oval, sessile to clasping, and have a somewhat hairy undersurface. The example shown was growing in mid-September alongside Thorburn Road on the outskirts of St. John's.

4. TRUE FORGET-ME-NOT
(*Myosotis scorpioides*)

Cymes of sky-blue petals and yellow centres, typically on paired stalks, atop square 1–2 ft. stems. Note the small white filaments radiating from the centre between each petal.

Leaves are untoothed, lance-shaped, and diminish in length up the stem. Commonly found as extensive masses of bloom in wet soils and along river banks. Those shown were growing in mid-June in the flood plain of a river through Bowring Park. A flower and spiked fruit of Common Buttercup (*Ranunculus acris*) are also seen in the photograph.

5.   SMALLER FORGET-ME-NOT
   (*Myosotis laxa*)

Small pale mauve to blue flowers on paired, relatively long cymes atop short, sturdy, leafy stems. Flowers may also occur on minor cymes arising from leaf axils. The plant

spreads by creeping stems radiating from the base of established plants. Leaves are long-oval, alternate and sessile. The examples shown were growing at the edge of a shallow, mud-bottomed pool at Jack's Pond Camping Park in late-August.

6.   FIELD FORGET-ME-NOT
   (*Myosotis arvensis*)

Racemes of small, dull-blue, white centred flowers atop square hairy stems a foot or more high. Stem branches arise from axils of equally hairy, long-elliptical, alternate leaves. The example shown was growing in our backyard in mid-June.

37. MINT FAMILY
(*Labiatae*)

Flowers of various shapes having 5 petals, usually fused into a trumpet, terminating in an upper "hood", lower "lip", and two side "ears". A typical flower has 4-stamens (sometimes only 2) and a single pistil. Stems are usually square in cross-section.

1.   CUT-LEAVED WATER
   HOREHOUND
   (*Lycopus americanus*)

Pairs of sharply pointed and distinctly toothed leaves regularly spaced along the stem, with successive leaf pairs set at right angles to each other. Small white tubular flowers are clustered in the axils. The plant grows to a height of 2 feet or more in wet soil. The example shown was growing in a ditch alongside the route of the old railway track through Whitbourne in mid-August.

2.   WOUNDWORT
   (*Stachys palustris*)

Whorls of lipped, eared and hooded magenta flowers project from a basal ring of 5 stiff, brown, sharply pointed sepals. These whorls are bunched at leaf axils on the upper portion of the ridged or cornered, slightly hairy stem. The flower lip is patterned with white circles. Leaves are paired, sessile, lance-shaped, toothed and downward curving. Those above the lowest whorl of flowers are

generally smaller and tinted brown. The example shown was about 2 feet tall, growing beside the Quidi Vidi Walking Trail near Rennie's River in early-September. Note that, when pollinated, the petal tube drops from the sepals (calyx). A fly has begun investigating one of the flowers.

3.   LAMBS EARS
   (*Stachys lanata*)

A close relative of *S. palustris*, Lambs Ears has purple flowers and a prominent coating of white fuzz. It is widely grown as a garden plant but is not yet a common "escape". It is included here for comparison and as an item of interest. It was photographed in late-August at the Botanic Park on Mount Scio Road, St. John's.

4.   COMMON SKULLCAP
   (*Scutellaria epilobiifolia*)

A pair of lipped and hooded, purple and white flowers project from the axils of each pair of leaves along its ridged or square stem.

36-5

36-6

37-1

37-2

37-3

Quidi Vidi–Rennie's River Walking Trail:
Here a pedestrian bridge crosses Rennie's River along the walkway from Quidi Vidi Lake to Pippy Park, a distance of 1.5 miles (2.5 km).

37-4

37-5   37-6   37-7

37-8 ***Public wharf at Mary's Harbour (Pop. 450):***
Service centre for several communities unconnected by road.

37-9   37-10   37-10A

The example was growing in late-August at Backside Pond Provincial Park.

5. HEART MINT
(*Mentha cardiaca*)
Thick whorls of lavender to pale violet flowers in the axils of downward-curving, broadly elliptical, finely toothed leaves. Protruding stamens give the flower whorls a prickly appearance. Usually found in large colonies along river banks. The specimens shown were growing in the shallow foreshore of a pond near Whitbourne in mid-August. Note the tendency of the down-curved leaves to overlap the leaf below.

6. WILD MINT
(*Mentha arvensis*)
Similar to *M. cardiaca* but its stem is deep purple. Pairs of leaf-like stipules (which may be newly arising branches) occur at lower leaf axils. Leaves are not as strongly down-curving as in *Mentha cardiaca*. The example shown were growing alongside Rennie's River opposite Confederation Building in mid-September.

7. CREEPING CHARLIE/GILL-OVER-THE-GROUND/GROUND IVY
(*Glechoma hederacea*)
Lipped, eared and hooded magenta flowers project in 2's or 4's from a vertical stem at axils of paired, brownish, kidney-shaped leaves having a blunt-toothed or scalloped edge. The photograph was taken in mid-July at Green Point in Gros Morne National Park, about 6 miles north of the Town of Rocky Harbour. We had walked along the shore accompanied by our dog Kala, a Newfoundland / English Setter cross, to see the contorted rock formations. Having arrived on the north side of the Point we decided to climb the cliff and walk back to the parking area by way of the upper meadowland. The climb up the cliff was not so easy for Kala. However, being a gentle and cooperative dog, we eventually jointly managed the ascent. On the way back across the meadowland we came upon the remnant foundations of an old homestead. It was among these that a large colony of Creeping Charlie was flourishing.

8. HEAL-ALL/SELFHEAL
(*Prunella vulgaris*)
A low-lying flower, not usually exceeding 6 inches in height. Stems tend to extend laterally from the root and then turn upwards. Purple flowers typical of the family, but with a finely fringed lip, occur in a whorled terminal spike, the bracts forming a cone-shaped structure. The photograph was taken in mid-August at Jack's Pond Provincial Park.

9. BUGLE
(*Ajuga reptans*)
Blue to purple flowers in whorls typical of the family, except that the petal forming the hood is small. Leaves are paired, roundish and slightly scalloped. Lateral growth by runners rooting at leaf nodes. Specimens shown were growing in early July beside a small brook trickling down a steep hillside at Bowring Park, St. John's.

10. HEMP-NETTLE
(*Galeopsis tetrahit*)
Pink to purple, trumpet-shaped flowers project from spikey calyx whorls at the axil of paired leaves. Leaves are broadly oval or elliptical and are coarsely toothed along the outer edge. Stems are bristly-hairy. Secondary stems are paired and divergent from the main stem. The petal forming the hood of the flower is conspicuously hairy. The mid-lobe of the lower lip is notched and has a yellow palate. The example shown was growing at Mary's Harbour, Labrador in late-August.

10A.
This white-flowered variety of Hemp Nettle was photographed at Black Tickle, Labrador a day or two later.

38. NIGHTSHADE FAMILY
(*Solanaceae*)

An economically important family which includes potatoes, tomatoes, peppers and tobacco, and some commonly used ornamentals such as petunias. With a few notable exceptions, such as potatoes, most species are tropical or require a warmly temperate climate. Some berries or seeds of Nightshades are poisonous, some notoriously so, such as Jimson Weed (*Datura stramonium*); Henbane (*Hyocyamus niger*); Deadly Nightshade (*Atropa belladonna*). None of these particular three species are known to occur here. Flowers are radially symmetrical, usually 5-parted with petals joined, sometimes only at the base, forming a bell-shape. Fruit may be a seed capsule or a green berry turning red, yellow or black when ripe. Leaves are usually relatively large and alternate. Flowers may occur singly or on a branching flower-stalk (cyme) arising from leaf axils or directly from the stem of the plant.

1. CLIMBING NIGHTSHADE/ BITTERSWEET
(*Solanum dulcamara*)

A 5-part flower with pale mauve to deep reddish-purple, sharply pointed petals carried on a few- to many-flowered cyme arising directly from the stem of the plant. As each flower matures the petals eventually assume a fully-reflexed position exposing the bright yellow "beak" formed by the large-anthered stamens pressed together in the centre forming a cone around the style. It is a climbing or "scrambling" plant, woody at the base but herbaceous in its seasonal growth. Leaves are simple but strongly eared or lobed at the base and have straight edges. Where leaf-lobes are large, a secondary and smaller pair of lobes may occur. The fruit is a green berry at first, turning bright red when ripe. The example shown was growing in mid-September in our backyard. A small thicket of these regularly thrives near the Health Sciences Centre Heating Plant on MUN Campus, St. John's.

39. SNAPDRAGON FAMILY
(*Scrophulariaceae*)

Flowers constructed of 5 variously united or partly united petals forming a tube, sometimes hooded and usually 2-lipped. Stamens may vary in number from 2 to 5. Some members of the Snapdragon Family are "hemiparasites", in that they develop a root system sufficient only to tap into the root system of neighbouring plants from which they draw water and minerals. These they transform into their food requirement (sugars) themselves by photosynthesis enabled by the chlorophyll contained in their own green leaves. They are therefore not fully parasitic. These include the genera *Euphrasia* (Eyebright), *Digitalis* (Foxglove), *Castilleja* (Painted-cup), *Rhinanthus* (Rattle), *Pedicularis* (Lousewort).

1. EYEBRIGHT
(*Euphrasia spp.*)

Euphrasia is a small variable genus, usually no more than a foot high and often only a few inches, recognized by its 3-lobed purple-streaked lower petal (each lobe notched) and the small hood formed by its fused upper two petals. Its paired, sessile, stubby, fan-shaped and prominently-toothed leaves are also a distinguishing feature. The example shown is a white, much-branched, bushy species, probably *E. americana*, its leaves sharply toothed and flowers in axils of the upper leaves. It was growing in late August at Backside Pond

38-1

39-1

39-1A

Sasha:
Clipped for summertime comfort, Sasha rests among Blue Bead Lillies while watching her family.

Our Dogs:
Our Newfoundland Dog, Sasha, with her daughter, Kala, beside her at Backside Pond Camping Park.

39-1B

39-2

39-3

Trout River:

The fishing community of Trout River nestled below a glacial ridge of fine gravel at the southwest extremity of Gros Morne National Park.

39-4

39-5

39-6

Provincial Park, located on the east side of Trinity Bay, south of Heart's Content.

We have found this to be a very pleasant park, mainly because of its interesting walking trails. We have often visited the Heart's Content Museum, commemorating the landing of the first successful trans-atlantic cable there on July 27, 1866. Each time we find something new has been added to a quite interesting presentation of those historic times.

1A.
A dominantly single-stemmed species, probably Stiff Eyebright (*E. rigidula*). Stem and leaves are deep red, leaves so sharply toothed that they may be termed "bristley". Note that the flowers are also strongly marked in deep red. These were growing in August in the flood-plain of the river through Jack's Pond Provincial Camping Park. Note the Sundew and other nearby water-associated plants.

1B.
A smaller, less foliated, more weakly stemmed Eyebright. The flower has a yellow throat and purple-lined petals, probably *E. randii*. It was growing in my back yard in August.

2. FOXGLOVE
(*Digitalis purpuria*)
A tall single stem up to 6 ft. high bearing a one-sided spike of large, tubular, nodding, pink or white flowers having a slightly extended lower lip. In pink varieties the spotted nature of the lower inside portion of the flower tube is readily apparent and is thought to be a feature attractive to bees. This is also present in white flowers but is of differing reflective quality undifferentiated by colour, thus indicating that bees see differently than we do. Leaves are large, spearshaped, stalked, finely toothed and softly downy. Foxgloves occur as garden escapes and have been escaping for some consider-

able time. The example shown was growing beside the Southern Shore Highway near Tors Cove in mid-August.

3. TURTLEHEAD
(*Chelone glabra*)
A cluster of white bulbous, two-lipped flowers at the top of 2–3 ft. stalks. Leaves are paired, broad lanceolate, toothed and pointed. Usually found in wet, poorly drained locations. Those shown were growing in a hollow along a woods path at Lady Pond, north of Smith Sound, in early-August.

4. NORTHERN PAINTED-CUP
(*Castilleja septentrionalis*)
Greenish-yellow flowers in a terminal cluster supported by similar colour bracts shading to a reddish brown at the tips. Narrow, pointed, bronze-coloured, untoothed leaves alternate along a smooth, dark brown stem and are broader at the summit. Flowers shown were about 8 inches tall and were growing in late-July about halfway up the side-slope of The Tablelands on the road to Trout River in Gros Morne National Park.

5. VELVET BELLS/ALPINE
     BARTSIA
     (*Bartsia alpina*)
A cluster of deep purple, tubular flowers with a slightly whitened, hairy surface terminating an erect, purplish unbranched, hairy and squared stem up to 10 inches high. Leaves are hairy, pointed-oval, sessile and edged with shallow-rounded teeth, the toothed edge also being tinged purple. A pair of flowers also occurs in the leaf axils immediately below the terminal cluster. Sepals and terminal leaves are the same colour as the petals. Note that the cream-coloured stamen tips barely extend from the mouth of the flower tube, but are readily apparent by the strong contrast of colour. The examples shown were growing in damp ground by a river bank near Cape Norman at the northern tip of the Great Northern Peninsula in mid-July.

49

6. BUTTER-AND-EGGS/TOADFLAX
(*Linaria vulgaris*)

A common sight in dry wasteland and roadsides from mid-August through September. A spike of pale yellow snapdragon flowers with an orange palate and downward projecting spur. An abundance of narrow, linear leaves arise from the stalk throughout its length. The specimen shown was about 1½ ft. high growing in our backyard. Note the somewhat thicker strap-like leaves along the upper portion of the squared main stem, extending into the flower spike.

6A.

A specimen with a branched inflorescence, more like a corymb than a raceme or spike, found growing near my home in late-August.

7. COARSE/GIANT TOADFLAX
(*Linaria dalmatica*)

Growing to 3 ft. or more it is much taller than Butter and Eggs. Its flowers are entirely lemon coloured. Leaves are broad at the base and clasp the stem. The example shown was growing on a narrow strip of wasteland lying between the highway and the protected inner waters of Bonne Bay in Gros Morne National Park.

8. OLD-FIELD/BLUE TOADFLAX
(*Linaria canadensis*)

A slender, sparsely branched plant bearing a raceme of pale blue to white, 2-lipped, short-spurred flowers atop the main stem. Flowers occur on branches only in a minor way. Leaves are linear, few, and may easily be mistaken for Brook Lobelia (*Lobelia kalmii*) except for the flower spur and the more prominent 2-humped white palate. The example shown was growing in mid-July beside Leary's Brook, St. John's, where it flows into Long Pond.

9. STRIPED TOAD FLAX
(*Linaria repens*)

Finely marked, mauve-striped flowers on separate, leafy flower stalks. Leaves are narrow and linear but occur more densely along the stem. The most prominent aspect of the flower is the hood formed by its three upper petals. The lip petal is not so prominent and the spur either absent or very short. Note that the palate retains a slight yellow tinge. This specimen was growing in mid-September near the foot-bridge over Rennie's River, St. John's.

9A.

A small, recumbent example with white, snapdragon-type flowers in a raceme at the end of a weak stem. Flowers of the raceme are grouped in fours. Leaves are sparse, small and linear. This specimen was also growing in September near Rennie's River Pedestrian Bridge.

9B.

White snapdragon-type flowers having a short spur but no yellow dot apparent on the palate, borne on firmly upright stems as interrupted racemes along the upper portion of the main stem, or as terminal clusters on secondary branches. Leaves are narrow, linear, in whorls of 3 or 4 and with small stipules in leaf axils. These were growing in September near the helicopter landing pad at the rear of the Health Sciences Centre, St. John's.

10. NARROW LEAVED YELLOW RATTLE
(*Rhinanthus stenophyllus*)

This wondrous world is full of life,
So rampant, robust, rare and rife,
Its beauty in majestic scale
And symmetry in fine detail.

A moment in evolution's chain
Is sum and substance of a plant's domain.
Survival is a life-long battle.
And so it is with the Yellow-Rattle.

It roots and sprouts; it lives and grows;
Strives to achieve before it goes.
The world moves on; the bees retire;
A wintery blast puts out the fire.

Its strings of life wrapped up in seed
Are stored for future lives to read.
What once a Yellow Rattle wore
Could be a Golden Troubadour.

39-6A

39-7

39-8

39-9

39-9A

39-9B

39-10

Cow Head:
Lobster pots neatly stacked after the close of the lobster season at Cow Head.

39-11

39-12

39-13

39-14

39-15

Yellow snapdragon flowers with a finely brown-mottled lower lip project from purple-tinged clam-shell sepals in the axils of the upper leaves. When seeds are formed they are encased by the sepals and rattle loosely within. Leaves are paired, pointed-triangular, sessile to slightly clasping the stem, and the toothed edges are made more prominent by incised marking on the surface of the leaves. The example shown was growing at Watt's Point Calcareous Barrens in mid-July.

11. MARSH RED-RATTLE
(*Pedicularis palustris*)
A dark, stick-like main stem with secondary stems arising from leaf axils. Small, fernlike, pinnate leaves occur on primary and secondary stems. Deep pink, tubular and lipped flowers also arise from leaf axils. A small forest of these plants was growing in late July in a wet roadside ditch at Cow Head.

The Town of Cow Head is a municipal enclave within Gros Morne National Park. It originated as a fishing village in one of the few natural harbours along the coastline north of Bonne Bay. We were favourably impressed by the nearby Shallow Bay Camping and Picnicking Park – its large camping sites and its wide expanse of sandy beach. Being budding naturalists, we were also attracted to the Park's wetlands where we saw our first Red-Winged Blackbird, not then included in Gros Morne's list of natural inhabitants.

12. FIERY LOUSEWORT
(*Pedicularis flammea*)
What at first appeared to be a plant which had succumbed to insect infestation or viral blight, on closer inspection prompted by the number of occurrences in the vicinity, turned out to be Fiery Lousewort having passed its flowering stage. Note the dark bronze, pinnate leaves and multiple fleshy stalks, red at the base. Those described by A. E. Porsild, are yellow snapdragon-types with red markings. The example shown was growing at

Watt's Point Calcareous Barrens in mid-July. We must have been so taken with this odd-looking plant (about 8 inches in height) that the little yellow flower opening in the foreground and the two lumpy-racemed stalks slightly behind the Lousewort and to either side, went completely unnoticed.

13. COW WHEAT
(*Melampyrum lineare*)
2-4 Tightly packed, multi-flowered clusters of yellow snapdragon-type flowers atop stiffly erect, few-branched, whitened or sparsely hairy stems up to 2 ft. high. Terminal clusters are closely back to back, each cluster backed by a whorl of green leaf-like bracts. The outer tip of each flower is yellow, turning brown on maturity. The base of the flower is a fuzzy pale greenish-yellow, becoming white on maturity. A whorl of 6–8 narrow leaf-like bracts occurs at branch junctions. The single to few stem leaves are pinnate with 8–12 narrow lance-shaped untoothed leaflets. The examples shown were growing in profusion between the road to Indian Head Park and the Stephenville Airport in mid-July.

14. COMMON SPEEDWELL
(*Veronica officinalis*)
Racemes of pale lavender 4-petalled flowers arising from the axils of large, paired, elliptical, finely toothed leaves on creeping stems. Note the pair of club-ended stamens projecting from the flower, and the hairy flower stem. The picture was taken in mid-July beside the walking trail around Berry Hill Pond, Gros Morne National Park.

15. BIRD'S-EYE/GERMANDER SPEED WELL
(*Veronica chamaedrys*)
Similar to *V. officinalis*, but has blue petals with a white centre and an erect slender stem arising from paired, heart-shaped leaves. The example shown was photographed near Tors Cove, on the Southern Shore Road to Trepassey, in mid-August.

16. AMERICAN BROOKLIME
(*Veronica americana*)

Small, violet to lilac, equal- and 4-petalled flowers in racemes arising from axils of sessile to clasping, slightly toothed, paired upper leaves. Lower stem leaves are short-stalked. Mature flowers project from the raceme on long thin stalks. The example shown was growing on the trail to Baker's Brook Falls in Gros Morne National Park in mid-July. Note the long, pointed-oval leaves and smooth (hairless) stem.

17. MARSH SPEEDWELL
(*Veronica scutellata*)

A Veronica with long-stalked flowers drooping from the raceme. Leaves are long, lance-shaped and sharp-toothed (sometimes untoothed). The example shown was growing beside Green Gardens Trail in Gros Morne National Park in the latter part of July.

40. PITCHER PLANT FAMILY
(*Sarraceniaceae*)

A small family of plants in which the leaves have been modified to a tubular form containing water into which the leaf exudes digestive enzymes. Insects attracted into the leaf opening and into the liquid contained therein are digested to supplement the plant's nutritional needs. Only one species, *Sarracenia purpurea*, occurs in the province and this has been adopted as the Province's floral emblem.

1. PITCHER-PLANT
(*Sarracenia purpurea*)

A 5-part, rather large, globular, solitary, nodding flower having dark-red to deep-wine petals and sepals on a smooth, green to reddish stem up to 1¹/₂ ft. tall, rising from a basal rosette of succulent, green to reddish, red-veined, tubular leaves having a collar or hood surrounding the open end of the tube or "pitcher". Plants may be solitary or in clumps growing in marshy locations. Two examples are shown:

1A.

Showing a clump of Pitcher Plants which still retain their red petals in mid-July. These were growing on a marsh beside the highway on the isthmus of the Avalon Peninsula.

1B.

Showing a single plant in mid-August, the petals having fallen revealing the large, green umbrella-shaped, 5-segment stigma. Note that the rosette of basal leaves have by this time turned a deep wine-purple colour. This specimen was growing in a marsh beside Seal Cove River, Conception Bay.

41. BLADDERWORT FAMILY
(*Lentibulariaceae*)

Insectivorous plants of aquatic or wetland habitat, otherwise closely related to the Snapdragon Family (*Scrophulariaceae*). Flowers are bilaterally symmetrical, 2-lipped, usually spurred, and either solitary or as sparse racemes on naked stems. Basal leaves designed for aquatic and insectivorous sustenance.

1. BUTTERWORT
(*Pinguacula vulgaris*)

Purple, 2-lipped flowers (lower lip 3-lobed, upper lip 2-lobed), fused behind the lips forming a tube which extends back as a spur beyond the 5 clasping, dark-purple sepals. Each flower is borne singly on 3–5 inch, erect, leafless, dark-purple stems covered

39-16   39-17   40-1B

40-1A

Conception Harbour:
A secluded anchorage in Conception Bay.

41-1

Point Riche:
*Rounded formations of conglomerate rock in the
Point Riche shoreline, between Port Aux Choix and
the lighthouse.*

41-2

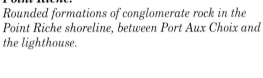

41-3

41-4

42-1

with short hairs. Numerous greenish-yellow, pointed oval to elliptical leaves with curled edges form a basal rosette. These leaves are fleshy and secrete a slime trapping insects which land on them. The leaf then rolls up and the insect is digested and absorbed as plant nutrient. The example shown was growing in mid-July at Point Riche on the west coast of the Great Northern Peninsula.

2. HORNED BLADDERWORT
(Utricularia cornuta)
Sunny-yellow, usually paired, 2-lipped, long-spured flowers, back to back atop a straight, erect, naked stem up to 6 inches tall. The lower lip is large, round, horizontal and greatly inflated in the centre forming a very prominent palate. The upper lip is fan-shaped and turned vertically upwards behind the palate. The spur or horn projects downward from the back of the flower and may be as long as or longer than the lower lip. The sepals enclosing the flower when in bud turn nut-brown, dry up and fall off early in the flowering process. The plant is terrestrial in muddy locations, its narrow, grass-like leaves usually buried in the mud. The example shown was growing in mid-August on a marsh near Seal Cove River, upstream from the Conception Bay Highway.

3. GREATER BLADDERWORT
(Utricularia vulgaris)
A similarly sunny-yellow but aquatic flower in a few-flowered raceme atop 8-10 inch stems. The flower has a broad, pointed lower lip and an upright, hood-shaped upper lip. The spur (not visible in the photograph) is shorter than in *U. cornuta* and curves forward beneath the lower lip. Flowers project from the stem on short alternating stalks. A small bract occurs at the juncture of each flower stalk with the stem. Basal leaves are adapted to an aquatic environment and are comprised of long-stalked finely dissected leaves with small bladders interspersed among the feathery leaflets. When activated by touch of a small insect the bladder opens and sucks the insect inside to be absorbed by the plant. The example shown was growing in early-August at Indian Arm Pond, a short distance eastward along the Trans-Canada Highway from Lewisporte Road junction.

4. INTERMEDIATE BLADDERWORT
(Utricularia intermedia)
Similar to *U. vulgaris* but having a somewhat smaller flower and the bladders occur on separate leaf stalks from the finely dissected, feathery leaflets. The example shown was growing in late-July in a backwater section of Seal Cove River, downstream from the Conception Bay Highway. Bladder-bearing leaves, as well as feathery leaves, are visible in the upper portion of the photograph.

42. PLANTAIN FAMILY
(Plantaginaceae)
Tight clusters or spikes of small inconspicuous flowers rising on unbranched stems from a basal rosette of oval to grass-like parallel-veined leaves. Stamens sometimes project noticeably from the flowers.

1. COMMON PLANTAIN
(Plantago major)
Long, tight spikes of greenish inconspicuous flowers rising above a basal rosette of broad-oval, strongly parallel-veined leaves. The tiny flowers are comprised of 4 green sepals and 4 membranous petals. The stamens, which may sometimes be seen protruding from the flowers, have purple anthers on the end of relatively long filaments. The example shown was growing in early-September in the backyard of a house in one of the older sections of St. John's.

2. SEASIDE PLANTAIN
(*Plantago maritima*)

Tight, inconspicuous, greenish flower spikes (not as long as *P. major*) rising on sturdy, slightly hairy stems from a basal agglomeration of narrow, fleshy leaves. The conspicuous stamens have yellow anthers on white filaments. Note also that pairs of small knobs or barbs occur along the edge of each leaf. The example shown was growing in mid-July on one of the arches at The Arches Scenic Site.

"The Arches" are eroded remnants of earlier coastline and are located northward along the highway from Gros Morne National Park.

3. ENGLISH PLANTAIN
(*Plantago lanceolata*)

A short flower spike atop a smooth, green, leafless stem up to 1 ft. tall, rising well above a basal rosette of oval to lance-shaped leaves. As the flowers mature from the base of the flower spike up-wards, the white-anthered stamens project outwards forming a tutu-like skirt around the spike. The example shown was growing in late-July on the edge of a roadway on the high land east of Stephenville, overlooking the town.

43. HONEYSUCKLE FAMILY
(*Caprifoliaceae*)

A relatively small family of shrubs, vines and a few herbs. Some common garden varieties include honeysuckles, weigelas and viburnums. Flowers may be bilaterally or axially symmetrical, usually 5-parted with petals fused forming a bell-shape or tube. Ends of the petals are lobed, sometimes deeply divided, forming a lipped appearance. Leaves are opposite and may be simple or divided. Fruit is a berry.

1. TWINFLOWER
(*Linnaea borealis*)

A low, creeping, mat-forming plant from which leafy shoots and flower stems arise. Flowers are in the form of paired, nodding, pink, 5-lobed bells diverging at the top of slender bare stems up to 6 inches high. Leaves are round to oval, paired, usually toothed on the leading edge, and are confined to the lower extremity of the flower stem and along the woody creeper. The example shown was growing beside the James Callahan Trail leading to Gros Morne, Gros Morne National Park in mid-July. The Twinflower has been adopted as the floral symbol for Oxen Pond Botanic Park, St. John's.

2. NORTHERN BUSH HONEYSUCKLE
(*Diervilla lonicera*)

A spreading, woody shrub growing to 4 ft. high. It has paired, short-stalked, sharply pointed, elliptical to ovate, finely toothed leaves. Flowers are 5-parted. The greenish-yellow to orange or scarlet petals are fused forming a tube with raggedly spreading and usually reflexed petal tips, allowing the stamens and the green-balled, long-styled pistil to be fully exposed. Flowers occur in clusters of 2 or 3 at the ends of branches and in upper leaf axils. The example shown was growing in late-July in the Seal Cove River flood plain, downstream from the hydro-generating plant. Normally, leaves are a dark green but in this instance many had turned dark brown. The cause of this is unknown, but may be related to soil conditions.

3. NORTHERN FLY HONEYSUCKLE
(*Lonicera villosa*)

A low woody shrub, sometimes erect to 3 feet or more and sometimes creeping, depending on the protective or exposure quality of the

42-2   42-3   43-1

Oxen Pond Botanic Park:
Located on Mt. Scio Road, a bronze plaque
at the park entry depicts the Park's
twinflower symbol.

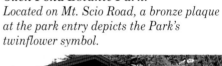

43-2

43-3

43-4

44-1

Colonial Building, St. John
This building housed the Newfoundland Legislature during the period 1850–1960. At present it houses the Provincial Archives.

St. John's Court House:
The Court House in downtown St. John's, as seen from Duckworth Street.

45-1

immediate environment. Leaves are elliptical to oval, and are paired along the woody stem. A whorl of leaves terminates each branch and is the first to appear in Spring. The 5-part flowers are paired on short flower stalks arising from leaf axils. Petals are pale yellow, fused at the base and 5-lobed. Stamens and pistil project to the extremity of the petal lobes. Its fruit is a dark blue, juicy and edible berry, ripening by late-July. The example shown was growing in mid-June beside the road to Cape St. Mary's Bird Sanctuary, near the highway junction. We have also found it in its creeping form flowering in early-June at Watt's Point Calcareous Barrens.

4. RED ELDERBERRY
(*Sambucus pubens*)
A woody shrub usually about 6 ft. high, but may occasionally exceed 10–12 ft. Flowers form a dense creamy-white pyramidal cluster (cyme) arising from leaf axils on sturdy, smooth, pale-green stalks. Each flower has 5 stubby, pointed, cream petals and a white, bulbous, central stigma surrounded by 5 projecting pale-yellow stamens. Leaves are opposite, pinately compound and divided into 4–6 lance-shaped, finely toothed, short-stalked, paired leaflets and a terminal leaflet. Fruit are bright-red berries (drupes). The example shown was growing at Indian Head Park, Stephenville in early-July.

44. TEASEL FAMILY
(*Dipsacaceae*)
A small family of plants somewhat similar to the Daisy Family (*Compositae/Asteraceae*). It has a flowerhead of many small florets subtended by a ring of bracts. These florets are tubular and bilaterally symmetrical, made up of 4–5 fused and lobed petals. Only 1 species of 1 genus – Field Scabious (*Knautia arvensis*) – is recorded in Rouleau's List Of Newfoundland Plants.

1. FIELD SCABIOUS
(*Knautia arvensis*)
Flat to slightly convex, mauve-coloured, round flowerheads terminating long, few-leaved, hairy, sometimes reclining stems. The outer tubular florets have elongated outer petal lobes giving the appearance of ray florets. Main leaves are deeply lobed, to the extent of appearing to be pinnate, and occur in rosettes. Stem leaves are smaller, narrower and paired. The example shown is part of an extensive mass which were overhanging a ditch beside a road on the North side of Bay Bulls in early-August.

45. BELLFLOWER FAMILY
(*Campanulaceae*)
5-Part flowers with petals fused at the base forming an axially symmetrical bell-shape with 5 flaring lobes in most of the genera or a bilaterally symmetrical tube having a 2-lobed upper lip and 3-lobed lower lip as in the lobelia genus. (These latter are sometimes treated as a sub-family: *lobelioideae*, and sometimes as a separate family: *lobeliaceae*).

1. CREEPING BELLFLOWER
(*Campanula rapunculoides*)
Blue to mauve, 5-lobed, bell-like flowers droop singly on thin flower stalks arising from the axils of alternating, short-stalked to sessile, lance-shaped, toothed leaves. These leaves diminish substantially in size up the stem. 5 Narrow green sepals project star-

like around the base of each flower and become reflexed as the flower matures. Basal leaves are stalked, heart-shaped and finely toothed. Many of these were growing as garden escapes in mid-July alongside the highway through Foxtrap, Conception Bay.

Doggeral on Development Dreams

*Flora and fauna ebb and flow
with changing environment.
The common man must come and go
to suit the establishment.
Environmental cycles were once a glacial pace.
When measured in millennia t'was not
a gruelling race.*

*But now establishment wields powers
once divine,
Subservient to technocrats who serve
the corporate shrine
And view progress in linear terms
of building on the past.
Reality shows "boom and bust"
to be the image cast.*

*The history of Foxtrap
may show this rather well.
The locals thought the railroad was
a corporate way to hell.
In 1881 and -2 they fought it
tooth and nail,
But finally were vanquished
by judicial threat of jail.*

*Then no one thought a highway was
a better way to go.
A century later rails are gone,
as dead as the old Dodo.
More recently the Foxtrap crowd
declined incorporation.
Establishment said piped service
must be their sole salvation.*

*Valued farmland now is scarce.
It may be gone tomorrow.
The fishery is worn thin.
Not now a base to borrow.
Flora, fauna, the common man.
There's not much left today.
Could progress next be skimming oil
out of Conception Bay?*

2. HAREBELL
(*Campanula rotundifolia*)

Violet-blue, bell-shaped, 5-lobed, nodding flowers with narrow, usually projecting sepals. Flowers nod from fine flower stalks arching from the upper extremity of a slender, wiry stem. Stem leaves are long, narrow and sessile, folded upwards along the edge forming a trough. Basal leaves are long-stalked, round and usually withered away by flowering time. The example shown was growing in mid- to late-July at Trout River Camping Park. A white-flowered variety of harebell (*Var. albiflora*) also occurs.

2A.

A 6-lobed, 6-sepaled harebell having only a single nodding flower on its stem. Stem leaves are long, spatulate to lance-shaped, flat, sparsely and shallowly toothed, relatively broad and numerous. The example shown was growing in mid-September at L'Anse au Clair on the south coast of Labrador near the Quebec-Labrador Boundary. Note that the rounded, stalked basal leaf is large and still remains at flowering time and that the narrow sepals are longer then in *C. rotundifolia*. It is growing among a ground cover of reindeer moss (*Cladonia spp.*).

3. WATER LOBELIA
(*Lobelia dortmanna*)

A sparsely-flowered raceme of nodding, pale violet, 5-lobed, tubular flowers atop a slender, leafless stem up to 18 inches or more high. The 3 lobes forming the lower lip of the flower are relatively broad and spreading. The upper 2 lobes are shorter, narrower and usually recurved. Short, linear, grass-like leaves form a rosette at the base of the stem. The example shown was growing at the shoreline of Southwest Pond, Salmonier Line in mid-August. Basal leaves are usually below water, and the red portion of the stem probably represents the depth of water during the earlier growth season.

45-2

45-2A

Conception Bay:
The estuary of Manuels River into Conception Bay. In the distance is Kelly's Island. Beyond it is Bell Island. The Town of Conception Bay South extends along the east side of the Bay and includes the communities of Topsail, Manuels, Foxtrap, Kelligrews, Upper Gullies and Seal Cove.

Rock Formation, L'Anse Au Claire:
Erosion of the surrounding rock cliff produces dramatic features as shown.

45-3

46-1   46-2   46-2A

46-3

Bonne Bay:
A view over Bonne Bay from atop The Tablelands.

The Tablelands:
Consoling our dog Kala who climbed with us to the top of The Tablelands. Gros Morne Mountain is seen in the centre distance.

46. COMPOSITE / DAISY FAMILY
(Compositae / Asteraceae)

Flowers typical of this family are composed of clusters of many small flowers (florets) tightly grouped together and supported by a cone-like receptical (involucre) formed by a ring or series of rings of modified leaves (bracts). Two types of florets are generally present, hence the term "composite", – a central disc of many tiny tubular florets (disc florets) surrounded by a ring of long flat florets (rays) which look like petals. However, variations exist to the exent that some members of the family have disc florets only, such as thistles; and some have ray florets only, as in dandelion.

1. CANADA THISTLE
(Cirsium arvense)

A pale mauve haze along the side of the road to Smith Sound Picnic Park (east of Clarenville in Trinity Bay) turned out to be an impenetrable mass of Canada Thistle 3–4 ft. tall. The flower is in the form of a dense cluster of thin, tubular disc florets (no ray florets) cupped at the base by an oval structure (involucre) made up of multiple rings of overlapping, tightly compressed bracts. The stout stems are ridged and smooth (not hairy). Leaves are stiff, undulating along the edges, and toothed, with sharp spines projecting from the teeth. It being a warm and sunny August day, the air was humming with the sound of bees, but none appear on the photograph.

2. SWAMP THISTLE
(Cirsium muticum)

This slender, solitary specimen appeared like a spark in the woods while exploring along a little rivulet into Lady Pond (north of Smith Sound). The surrounding growth was made up of alders and stunted spruce with a mossy groundcover. The flowers, two of which have gone to seed, stand atop a sparsely-leafed 4 ft. stem, generally smooth but with sporadic coarse hairs. Leaves clasp the stem and, unlike the Canada Thistle, are relatively soft with a hairy fuzz over the upper surface.

2A.

A stunted form of Swamp Thistle, no more than 1 ft. high, growing in late-July in the arid environment of The Tablelands, Gros Morne National Park. Its purple florets were not yet showing. However, the basal rosette of deeply lobed, stalked leaves is clearly apparent.

The climb from the parking area at the base of the mountain is quite strenuous because of the bouldery terrain, but very rewarding by way of magnificent views overlooking Bonne Bay. On reaching the summit we walked inland a ways, jumping from boulder to boulder, and picnicked on one of the many large flat-surfaced brown boulders which characterize the area. Surprisingly, flies were more numerous and bothersome on the summit than they were on the slope, leading us to wonder why this should be in the dry, rocky, almost vegetationless expanse of the tableland and not on the less arid slopes.

3. BULL THISTLE
(Cirsium vulgare)

As with other thistles, the flowerhead is formed of disc-florets only, which in Bull Thistle are a reddish-purple, and are cupped by a large, spherical spine-covered, involucre. The plant is well branched and may grow to 5 ft. from a rosette of lobed leathery leaves arising the previous year. The sturdy stem is hairy with continuous or intermittant wings tipped with stiff, yellow-spines. Leaves are long and leathery, and have sharply pointed, projecting lobes, also tipped with stiff, yellow spines. Flowerheads occur on leafed stalks arising from axils of the upper leaves. The example shown was growing in a vacant lot near our home in early September.

4. COMMON BURDOCK
(*Arctium minus*)

This photograph was taken in mid-July at the St. John's railway yard, in a sheltered location receiving reflected warmth from nearby stone and concrete buildings. There were quite a few of these growing in the vicinity, all about 5 ft. in height, quite bushy and about 3 ft. wide at the base. Note the succulent purplish stem and wide, soft leaves. When the flowerheads go to seed they form the well known "sticky bud" readily attaching to animal hair and clothing, thus spreading the seed.

5. BLACK KNAPWEED/HARDHEADS
(*Centaurea nigra*)

These grow all over the place, but seem to thrive best along the edge of public walkways. They are stalky and clumpy up to 2½ ft. high and have a tenacious root system. This particular specimen is looking its best and was photographed at the community park, Whitbourne, once the site of Sir Robert Bond's home, "The Grange", Circa. 1920. Bond (1857–1927) was Prime Minister of Newfoundland from 1900 to 1909.

6. CORNFLOWER
(*Centaurea cyanus*)

The similarity between Cornflower and Knapweed is apparent. However, the larger, more destinctive looking Cornflower with neater, more presentable foliage, has been commonly adopted into garden cultivation. It has disc florets only, but the outer florets are long, 2-pronged, blue rays. The flowers shown are garden "escapes" spreading freely along the roadside in early-July at Steady Brook on the Trans-Canada Highway east of Corner Brook.

7. SPINY-LEAVED SOW THISTLE
(*Sonchus asper*)

The sow thistle is a late-blooming weed (Sept.–Oct.) thriving on exhausted soil. It therefore recurs regularly on my front lawn, as attested by the photograph, growing to a height of 6 to 18 inches. Note the lance-shaped, spiney-toothed leaves clasping the smooth stem. The flower is similar to Hawkweed and goes to seed very quickly, seemingly overnight, with seed dispersal by the same kind of little white parachutes blowing in the wind.

8. COMMON ANNUAL/ SMOOTH SOW THISTLE
(*Sonchus oleraceous*)

More slender and usually taller than *Sonchus asper*, its alternating leaves terminate in a distinctive triangular form and have fringed leaf-stalks clasping the stem. Leaf margins may be toothed or lobed but are not spiney. The example shown was growing in early-September in the walkway alongside our backyard.

9. COMMON GROUNDSEL
(*Senecio vulgaris*)

What can be said of the groundsel,
Its flower so held in restrain
By tightly clasped sepals which keep it
Secure from the wind and the rain?

Its dandelion-stem is smooth and branched.
Its leaves like a double-barred cross.
One of the flowers has gone to seed
Showing its silky floss.

The picture was taken on Topsail Hill,
Overlooking Conception Bay.
Behind are Beggar-tick and Willow-herb
On this bright September day.

10. WOOD GROUNDSEL
(*Senecio sylvaticus*)

This little 10-inch groundsel is single-stemmed with small, alternating, regularly spaced, lobed leaves (may grow to 2 ft. or more). This species has an outer ring of very short ray florets, differing from Common Groundsel (*S. vulgaris*) which has tube florets only. Commonly occurring in disturbed waste land, this was photographed in July in my back yard.

46-4

46-5

46-6

46-7

46-8

46-9

46-10

46-11 46-12 46-13

46-15

46-14 46-14A 46-1

11. STINKING GROUNDSEL
(*Senecio viscosus*)

Growing in the St. John's Railway Yard, this specimen exhibits characteristics attributed to the "stinking groundsel", short yellow rays and somewhat hairy leaves and stem. However, no unusual odour was detected. It seems a pity that any flower should be called "stinking", considering that odour may well be to the nose as beauty is to the eye.

12. GOLDEN RAGWORT/
SPRING AVENS
(*Senecio aureus*)

The flowers pictured are part of a much larger group growing in mid-July in a marshy clearing off the trail to Baker's Brook Falls in Gros Morne National Park. We were attracted by only the slightest flicker of yellow showing through the trees bordering the trail, but on pushing through the bush we were rewarded with quite a spectacular array of these flowers growing to a height of 3 ft. or more. We have also seen a similar stand of these flowers growing alongside the road to Point au Mal, north of the Port au Port Peninsula isthmus. An identifying feature is the basal growth of heart-shaped leaves. Stem leaves are alternate, widely but equally spaced, sessile, spatulate in shape and coarsely toothed.

13. TANSY RAGWORT
(*Senecio jacobaea*)

The tansy ragwort is a fall wildflower, generally growing in large clumps. They present a brilliant yellow mass in the autumn sun and continue to give a sunny appearance even on dull days. Note the soft, fern-like leaves. The foliage may vary in colour from blue-green to yellow-green, depending on the soil environment. This photograph was taken just below the pedestrian bridge crossing Rennie's River while enjoying one of many pleasant strolls along the Quidi Vidi Walking Trail, St. John's.

14. ARNICA RAGWORT/
LEAFY RAGWORT
(*Senecio pseudo-arnica*)

This photograph was taken at Black Tickle, Labrador during a trip up the Labrador Coast to Nain on the coastal boat Northern Ranger. The flowers were about 1–1 1/2 ft. high and were spread over a large boggy area draining to the shoreline. Note the few-flowered terminal cluster atop an unbranched, succulent, leafy stem. Leaves are long-elliptical, bluntly and shallowly toothed, sessile and slightly rolled under at the edge.

14A.

The same species growing thickly in early-August on the shoreline of Trepassey at the southern tip of the Avalon Peninsula. Its leaves are similar to the former, but noticeably broader, wavey-edged and shiny. Note also the dense woolly coating around the flower buds and the greater number of flowers in the flower cluster. These were 3 ft. high or more on average.

15. PINEAPPLE WEED
(*Matricaria matricarioides*)

Sometimes referenced as *Chamomilla suaveolens*, these small plants (6–8 inches) were growing in our backyard in July. The leaves are soft and feathery. The flowerhead is a dome of greenish-yellow disc florets cupped by an involucre of bracts. The edge of the involucre may sometimes show a white sheath giving the appearance of vestigal white ray florets. As children we picked these flowerheads for a variety of purposes when playing "house", and our children have done the same with no direction from us. This seems to be a natural fate for these plants, yet they seem to have prospered and multiplied despite the onslaught of successive generations.

16. COMMON TANSY
(*Tanacetum vulgare*)

Clusters of button-like flowerheads of tightly packed, golden yellow disc florets atop branching stems up to 3 ft. tall. It has dark green, aromatic, pinnate leaves with many toothed leaflets. The example shown was growing in mid-October at the edge of a restaurant parking lot just west of Grand Falls-Windsor.

17. HURON TANSY
(Tanacetum huronense)

This is a maritime species found growing in mid-July at Watt's Point Calcareous Barrens on the Great Northern Peninsula. Note the usually single or paired, relatively large flowerhead of lemon-yellow disc florets with a few vestigial ray florets around the perimeter. Note also the whitened surface of the leafless stems. Soft, fern-like leaves arise separately from creeping roots and also have whitened stalks. This area is a natural botanic wonderland and a substantial portion has been designated as a protected environment.

18. COLTSFOOT
(Tussilago farfara)

*Single, sunny flowers
on thick-set stalks
Sparkle in the sunshine
on spring-time walks.
Yellow flowers poking from
the wintry ground.
Runner-roots form patches
where these are found.*

These were growing at the head of Long Pond, just north of Memorial University, in early-May. Note the thick scales along the otherwise leafless stem. Large, heart-shaped, stalked basal leaves arise after the flower goes to seed forming a "clock flower" similar to the Dandelion fuzz-ball. The immediate area is a well-known habitat for a wide variety of waterfowl throughout the year, but it also supports a remarkable variety of wildflowers.

The forested slope of Nagle's Hill to the north is also home to a large flock of crows whose regular daily activities are rather intriguing and perhaps worthy of study.

19. YELLOW SALSIFY
(Tragopogon dubius)

The flower opens with the morning sun, but closes again by the early afternoon. Its long sepal-like bracts are the most salient feature. The seed fuzz-ball is similar to that of the dandelion, but somewhat larger. The only place we have seen these growing is upstream from the head of Long Pond. The particular area in which they were growing has since been subject to landscaping associated with stream bed improvement. Their continued occurrence here is accordingly considered to be somewhat doubtful.

20. CANADA HAWKWEED
(Hieracium canadense)

Straight, leafy, unbranched, smooth stems up to 3 ft. or more in height having a branched terminal cluster of yellow flowers comprised of many straight-edged ray florets, serrated on the end. Leaves are sessile, lance-shaped, sharp-toothed, alternate and diminishing in size up the stem. The example shown was growing in mid-August near the Seal Cove Hydro Generating Station in Conception Bay.

It is difficult to differentiate among some of the hawkweed species because of the asexual manner of seed formation exhibited by many of them. This method of reproduction is called "apomixis", whereby flowers of some species are genetically capable of maturing to seed production without need of pollination. These breed true to form, as in vegetative reproduction, but with the additional capabilities of seed dispersal and dormancy enabled by seed propagation. The problem of species recognition, however, results from a retained ability to revert occasionally to sexual reproduction sometimes resulting in mutations which are then further propagated in mutated form by asexual seed formation.

46-17

46-18

46-19

Hotels:

Examples of hotel accommodation in St. John's and other urban centres. Radisson Plaza – now Delta St. John's – (right) and Hotel Newfoundland (below) are located in downtown St. John's. Both include a convention centre as do other hotels in St. John's, Corner Brook and Gander.

46-20

46-21   *46-22*   *46-22A*

Indian River:
Viewed from a prominence   *46-23*
within Indian River
Camping Park.

46-25   *46-24*

21. FLORENTINE KING DEVIL
(*Hieracium florentinum*)

A slender, sparsely-leafed, slightly hairy stem up to 3 ft. tall having a few-flowered, branched cluster of yellow-rayed hawkweed flowers. Its leaves are lance-shaped to spatulate, untoothed to few-toothed, and alternate up the stem. The example shown was growing in early-August at Indian River Camping Park on the Trans-Canada Highway west of the Springdale Road Junction. Indian River is a substantial but placid river flowing through birch and aspen forest. It parallels the highway for 12 miles from the Baie Verte Road junction to Springdale, but is well separated from it by distance and dense tree growth, preserving its wilderness tranquility. It is an ideal route for beginner canoeists.

22. COMMON HAWKWEED
(*Hieracium vulgatum*)

Panicles of yellow flowerheads terminating a stiffly erect, few-leafed, slightly hairy, green to reddish-purple stem up to 3 ft. or more in height. This species is extremely variable. Leaves occur mainly as a basal rosette but also on the lower stem and may be narrow to broadly lance-shaped, deeply and sharply toothed or shallowly lobed, sessile or stalked, and commonly purple mottled. The few stem leaves reduce in size up the stem and usually occur only at flowerhead stalk junctures. The example shown was growing in mid-August in a gravel-pit near the water intake for the flume to the hydro-generating station at Seal Cove, Conception Bay. These plants are commonly found growing in urban locations around the base of buildings and in vacant lots.

22A.

A second example is provided to show the variability of *H. vulgatum*. This specimen was growing in more verdant surroundings in the Community Park at Whitbourne in late-August. Note the uniformly green leaves and absence of flower stalks arising from the lower stem.

23. YELLOW HAWKWEED/ KING-DEVIL
(*Hieracium pratense*)

A tight cluster of yellow-rayed flowers atop a straight, unbranched, hairy, leafless stem, up to 3 ft. high. The rings of bracts at the base of each flower are dark and have black hairs. Leaves are long-eliptical to spatulate, pointed, hairy and form a basal rosette. The example shown was growing in mid-July at Manuels, Conception Bay, but is quite common throughout the island portion of the Province.

24. ORANGE HAWKWEED/ DEVIL'S PAINTBRUSH
(*Hieracium aurantiacum*)

Similar to Yellow-Hawkweed, but its tight terminal cluster of flowers are composed of vivid orange, square-tipped rays. It is also generally shorter (up to 2 ft. in height) and its bracts, stem and basal leaves are densely covered with black hairs. The example shown was growing in early-July at Barachois Camping Park. We had stopped here for lunch to let our dogs have a stretch when returning from a trip to Stephenville. It being mid-week and early in the season, we had the picnic section all to ourselves. There was quite an array of wildflowers in bloom at the time – veronica, iris, yellow and orange hawkweed – all looking "fresh as daisies".

25. MOUSE-EAR HAWKWEED
(*Hieracium pilosella*)

These are lemon-yellow, hawkweed-type flowers borne singly on 4–6 inch stems. The flowers open in bright sunshine, but close in the evening and on dull, overcast days. They encroach on lawns and gardens by extending runners over the ground, which, together with the low-lying leaves, tend to form a mat-like ground cover. The name is descriptive of the relatively small, ovate to elliptical, untoothed leaves which are covered by white hair on the underside. The example shown was growing in mid-July on the upper slope of Manuels River Canyon, near the river estuary into Conception Bay.

26. SEASIDE HAWKWEED
(*Hieracium marianum*)

A single, hairy and wiry-stemmed, lemon-yellow hawkweed having whorls of long, lance-shaped, untoothed, ascendent, clasping leaves on separate stems. Leaf mid-ribs are purple, and some leaves may be mottled purple or entirely purple. The flower does not exceed the height of the leaves. The example shown was growing in mid-July at the shoreline of Manuels River near its estuary into Conception Bay.

27. DWARF DANDELION/POTATO-DANDELION
(*Krigia dandelion*)

A single hawkweed-like flower, on a smooth, naked stem, growing from a clump of lettuce-like leaves around the base of the stem. This specimen was growing alongside the railroad track at Whitbourne in early July.

Whitbourne was a hub of railway activity during the early years of railway construction (Circa 1880). A length of track and a variety of railway cars and equipment reminiscent of the period are still maintained there by the Town Council.

28. COMMON DANDELION
(*Taraxacum officinale*)

Single, sunny-yellow, many-rayed flower-heads atop smooth, green or purple-tinted hollow stems up to a foot or more in height. Several stems may arise from the root. It has a thick basal rosette of long, deeply lobed and jagged leaves. Note also that the outer ring of bracts at the base of the flowerhead is strongly reflexed downwards. On close inspection a multitude of paired, divergent stigmas are seen arising from the centre of the flowerhead, and each ray has a pair of stamens attached to its base. Yet, with all this sexual capacity, the Dandelion's reproductive system is primarily "apomictic" (female cells mature to seed production without pollination). It is certainly a tenacious and adaptable plant. When our lawn is mowed regularly, the plant adapts to the low-cut environment by sending up buds which flower almost at ground level. In some local instances the flower has been called "dumble-dor", possibly a corruption of the French for "golden parasol". The French name for it is "pissenlit" and it is interesting to note that when we were young, dandelions were commonly referred to as "piss-the-beds". Bane to many a lawn-owner, the dandelion is a tenacious weed with roots extending deep into the soil. It is an early spring riser, particularly in the warmed soil around house foundations. When seeding it forms a white fuzz-ball and its seeds are borne far and wide by the wind. As children we called these "clock flowers", telling the time by the number of puffs required to blow the seeds from the stem. The example shown was growing in our back yard in late-June, indicative of its extended period of growth. Its bright yellow radiance boosts the spirit, especially in early spring. The young leaves, when boiled, are akin to spinach. On only one occasion have we had the opportunity to taste a wine made from the flower heads. It was a clear amber colour and quite palatable.

29. MARSH DANDELION
(*Taraxacum palustris*)

Single yellow-rayed, dandelion-type flower-heads atop a multitude of sturdy, smooth, green, leafless, reed-like stems up to 2 ft. high, occasionally branched. Leaves are basal, broad-oval, may be somewhat toothed or lobed, and have a tendency to be prostrate. The example shown was growing in mid-August on the bank of Seal Cove River below the Conception Bay Highway.

Whitbourne: *(Population 1,100)*
A hub of activity during railway construction years
(1880's), it is now a commercial/service centre for the
central Avalon area. (see also 46-5, p. 58)

46-26

46-27

46-29

The Foaming Sea:
A moment in the everchanging interplay of light,
waves and water translucence.

46-28

46-30   46-31   46-32

Long Range Mountains:
Looking southward from the service station mentioned in text of 46–31. This range extends the full length of the Island's west coast.

46-33   46-34   46-3

30. CAT'S-EAR
(*Hypochaeris radicata*)
Single yellow-rayed flowers, similar to but smaller than dandelion flowerheads, on slender few-branched stems up to 1½ ft. high. Small scale-like leaf stubs occur along the otherwise smooth stem. Long-lanceolate, deeply toothed or lobed leaves form a basal rosette. The example shown was growing at the same time and in the same general area of Seal Cove River as the Marsh Dandelion.

31. FALL DANDELION/HORSE DANDELION/HAWKBIT
(*Leontodon autumnalis*)
Similar to Cat's-Ear except that the underside of the outer ray florets are usually red-streaked, and basal leaves are narrower and even more deeply toothed or lobed. The example shown is not the common Fall Dandelion, but the variety "*ochroleuca*", described in Gray's Manual (Fernald) as having greenish-yellow flowerheads lacking outer ray florets and having a thickened stem below the flowerhead. Note the small dark bracts located around the thickened portion of the stem. These were growing in early-August at the edge of a service station lot near Port aux Basques.

32. NIPPLEWORT
(*Lapsana communis*)
Flowerheads comprised of relatively few (9–10) yellow ray florets only, in branching clusters on thin stalks arising from leaf axils alternating up a stiff, hairy stem. Leaves have a large, pointed oval, shallowly toothed, terminal lobe, and one to several smaller lobes along the winged leaf-stalk. The example shown was growing in the flood plain of Rennie's River, beside the Quidi Vidi Walking Trail, St. John's, in early September.

33. BIENNIAL HAWKSBEARD
(*Crepis biennis*)
Very similar in general appearance to Common Hawkweed, but its stem is greener and less hairy and its leaves less subject to mottling. It has few to many yellow flowerheads in a terminal corymb atop leafless to few-leaved, smooth to slightly hairy, sometimes forking stems up to 3 ft. high. Basal leaves are broad-oval to spatulate, with wavy to shallowly lobed edges. The example shown was growing at Bowring Park, St. John's in early-June.

34. BIENNIAL BLUE LETTUCE
(*Lactuca biennis*)
A loose, much-branched panicle of ragged, yellow-rayed flowerheads, the rays being quite narrow and threadlike. Small, lance-shaped leaves clasp the upper stem. Basal leaves are like dandelion leaves but also have finely toothed edges. These were growing along the roadside skirting Bonne Bay in Gros Morne National Park in late July. We were driving along enjoying the many wide scenic vistas and it took a few seconds for the mind to register that there was a different sort of flower in the foreground. By the time we stopped there was a fair bit of reverse driving required to return to the spot. As often happens when stopping to take a closer look at a particular flower, we found other heretofore unseen flowers as well. A possible conclusion to be drawn from this is that, there being many places along provincial roadways that we have not stopped, there must be a myriad of different flower species and varieties still unseen. The mind is then led to dwell for a while on the infinite capacity of nature.

35. HAIRY LETTUCE
(*Lactuca hirsuta*)
The example shown was growing in early-August near the shoreline at Daniel's Point, Trepassey. It is a particular variety

(*Var. sanguinea*) named for the blood-red colour of the stem. Note the cylindrical dark-bracted buds and the large, densely compact, yellow flowerheads which occur in a terminal corymb-like cluster atop slightly hairy stems up to 3 ft. tall. Leaves are dandelion-like and are mainly basal or occur on the lower portion of the stem. A few small, narrow and sharply pointed, sessile, widely separated leaves occur on the upper part of the stem.

36. GALL-OF-THE-EARTH
(*Prenanthes trifoliolata*)
Clusters of drooping, bell-like white flowers with numerous long-styled stigmas projecting beyond the bell formed by the flower rays. Note the reddish stem and the broad, 3-part (hastate) lower leaves. These 1–3 ft. plants were growing in late-August on the top of Mount Scio in Pippy Park on the northern outskirts of St. John's. The summit of Mount Scio, at an elevation slightly above 500 ft. is a miniature rocky barrens having a southwesterly exposure to the elements from which there is a fine panoramic view of the northern half of St. John's.

36A.
A dwarf variety "*nana*", 6–8 inches tall, growing in late-August on the Hawk Hills, inland from Holyrood, Conception Bay.

37. WHITE LETTUCE/
RATTLESNAKE ROOT
(*Prenanthes alba*)
Much taller than Gall-of-the-Earth (*P. trifoliolata*), this specimen was 4-5 ft. in height growing alongside the railway track near Indian Arm Pond, Central Newfoundland in early July.

38. OX-EYE SUNFLOWER
(*Helianthus nuttallii*)
A dozen or more long, elliptical, sunny-yellow ray florets, each twice as long as the diameter of the flat, brownish disc. Leaves are very short stalked, finely toothed, usually paired,

and often show 3 nerves or veins at their base. Flowers occur singly atop wiry, purple stems up to 3 ft. high.

Many of the common wildflowers seen along the roadside are often assumed to be native to the province, but in reality were introduced accidentally by European settlers many years ago and have since become naturalized. This garden escape was growing on the edge of Thorburn Road, northeast of St. John's, in mid-September. The groundsel going to seed near the base of the plant, together with the pink knapweed and butter-and-eggs in the background make a colourful natural setting.

39. CORN CHAMOMILE
(*Anthemis arvensis*)
A daisy-like flowerhead with white ray florets and a domed yellow disc atop a smooth, branching stem up to 1 ft. tall. Leaves are feathery, much dissected, at the point of being threadlike, and are shorter and less numerous on the upper portion of the stem. The example shown was growing at the foot of Mt. Scio to the rear of the Health Sciences Centre, St. John's, in early-August. A very similar species, *Anthemis cotula*, (Mayweed) has sterile ray florets (neither stamens nor styles) and has a sharp pungency rather than being aromatic.

40. SCENTLESS CHAMOMILE
(*Tripleurospermum inodorum*)
The flowerhead is like *Anthemis arvensis* but ray florets are fewer (less then 20), narrower, and are usually more down-turned. Leaves are deeply dissected and thread-like but occur less densely along the stem, and are not strongly aromatic. This species is recorded in some references as a sub-species of *Matricaria maritima*, but recent, more detailed investigation has shown it to be more properly classed as a separate species. The pretty group shown was growing beside Rennie's River on the Quidi Vidi Walking Trail, St. John's in early-September.

46-36　　　　　　*46-36A*　　　　　　*46-37*

46-38

View from Mt. Scio: *(Pippy Park, St. John's)*
The Health Sciences Centre and Memorial
University Campus are to the right in the middle-
distance. Long Pond, with Confederation Building
beyond, is more distant to the left.

46-39　　　　　　　　　　　*46-40*

46-41

46-42

46-43

Trinity, Trinity Bay:
Site of the first Admiralty Court in North
America (1615), Trinity "... is perhaps the
most notable "heritage community," in the
Province". The picture shows St. Paul's
Anglican Church (rebuilt in 1892).

46-44

46-45

46-46

41. WILD DAISY
(Erigerin hyssopifolius)

This low-growing daisy (4–5 inches high) has 20–30 narrow, white, ray florets and a yellow disc. Its leaves are basal, lance-shaped, untoothed, and tend to fold under at the edge. The picture was taken in mid-July at Watt's Point Calcareous Barrens, now designated an ecological preserve.

42. WHITE-TOP FLEABANE
(Erigerin strigosis)

This daisy has 40 or more narrow white florets (count them). Its leaves are few, lanceolate and untoothed. We had stopped at Thorburn Lake Picnic Park, just north of Clarenville, in early August. It was a beautiful cloudless day, with only a slight occasional breeze. Ideal for canoeing! We packed a lunch, put the dogs in the canoe, and spent the rest of the day paddling around the perimeter of the lake, stopping to explore at any interesting or convenient landing place. The railway skirts the west side of the lake, bridging a shallow inlet at the northwest corner where a few summer cabins are located. The breeze dropped out completely and it became actually hot, so we stopped for lunch and found the White-Top Fleabane.

43. ENGLISH DAISY
(Bellis perennis)

Single white-rayed flowerheads, sometimes pink-tinged, atop short, (up to 6 inches) hairy, leafless, reddish stems. Basal leaves are oval to spatulate and may be untoothed or have 4–6 small teeth along the outer edge. It is a "gynodioecious" flower (some are female only, others hermaphrodite). The example shown was growing in mid-July at Point Riche, about half way up the Great Northern Peninsula.

44. OX-EYE DAISY/ BACHELOR'S BUTTON
(Chrysanthemum leucanthemum)

Petals blowing in the wind
and nodding as we pass.
Tiny, white-winged yellow doves
aflutter in the grass.
Nature's angels frolicking
in sunny summer mood.
God made the spritely daisy
and saw that it was good.

Long white ray florets (sometimes as many as 30) surrounding a button-like yellow disc. Few to many sparsely leafed stems, each with a solitary terminal flowerhead. Its leaves are sessile, relatively short and narrow, and may be deeply toothed or lobed. Those shown were growing in early-August behind the Health Sciences Centre, St. John's. They are prominent in their natural setting, growing among several species of clover.

45. COSTMARY/FEVERFEW
(Chrysanthemum parthenium)

A bushy, branching, broad-leafed, smooth-stemmed plant with numerous, terminal, daisy-like flowers having rays shorter and more rounded than the Ox-eye Daisy. Its pinnate leaves are lobed and fern-like. The example shown was blooming in mid-September near the Health Science Centre. It may sometimes be placed by taxonomists with the genus *Tanacetum* as *T. parthenium*.

46. SNEEZEWEED YARROW
(Achillea ptarmica)

The disc florets as well as the ray florets are white in this daisy-type flower. The disc is relatively large and rounded. Rays are few (8-12), stubby, and incline downwards from the disc. The leaves are long, narrow and pointed, with untoothed or finely toothed edges. The example shown was growing in early-September alongside an old cart track near Trinity, Trinity Bay.

Additional examples A. and B. are included here to demonstrate the variations that occur within this species.

46A.
Terminal clusters of stalked, small, round, white flowers (each about 7mm in diameter) atop 2¹/₂–3 ft. stems. Leaves are short, sessile, narrow lanceolate, untoothed or slightly toothed. These were growing in early-September on the riverbank of Rennie's River, south of the bridge on Elizabeth Avenue.

46B.
Somewhat similar to A. in general appearance, but only 6–8 inches in overall height. This specimen was growing in mid-June at Watt's Point Calcareous Barrens, well separated in time and place from Example A. Note the dahlia-like flower, slightly hairy stalk, and lance-shaped leaves with finely-toothed edges.

47. YARROW/DEADMAN'S DAISY
(*Achillia millefolium*)
A particularly hardy weed that is capable of flourishing under severe conditions. Its roots form a thick mat discouraging other growth. Leaves are deeply and extensively dissected, soft and fern-like. Flowerheads have broad white rays, sometimes lobed on the outer edge, and a central disc of dull white, tubed florets, in numerous, compact, flat-topped umbels. Those pictured were growing in late-September near Confederation Building, St. John's.

47A.
The pink variety of *A. millefolium* is less common than the white but is found all over nonetheless. The example shown, providing greater detail of flower structure, was growing in early-July at Marystown on a grassy prominence overlooking the shipyard.

48. PEARLY EVERLASTING
(*Anaphalis margaritacea*)
Clusters of small spherical separately stalked flowerheads, each encrusted with white papery bracts from which emerge a dense disc of yellow florets (female florets are on separate plants). Narrow, untoothed, pointed leaves alternate up the 2 ft. unbranched stems. Both stem and leaves are covered with fine white hairs, giving the plant a bluish-green appearance. The example shown was growing in early-September beside Prince Philip Parkway, St. John's.

49. SPATULATE PUSSYTOES
(*Antennaria spathulata*)
A terminal cluster of soft white disc florets (no ray florets) from which it gets the name "Pussytoes". The 6–8 inch stem is purplish, but whitened by a thick coating of soft white hairs. Stem leaves are long, narrow, ascending and clasp the stem. Basal leaves are spatulate with a rounded tip, untoothed, whitened on the undersurface, and tend to curve or bend upwards around the central vein of the leaf. The plant extends by surface runners forming a mat over the growing area. The example shown was growing in early-July atop Signal Hill, St. John's, the site of the first trans-Atlantic wireless transmission made by Guglielmo Marconi in 1901. Marconi was subsequently awarded the Nobel Prize for physics in 1909, thereafter continuing to develop the technology towards voice transmission, radio-directional navigation and radar.

50. WOODLAND CUDWEED
(*Omalotheca sylvaticum*)
Single to many powdery-white, unbranched stems up to a foot or more in height, each bearing a spike of brown-bracted flowerheads growing from leaf axils along the upper half of the stem. Leaves are narrow, single-veined, straight-edged, sessile and ascendant. This plant may sometimes be classified under the genus name *Gnaphalium*. The example shown was growing in early-September in the trailer park at Pippy Park on the north side of Long Pond, St. John's. The trailer park is quite usefully located, being within easy

46-46A   46-46B   46-47

46-48

46-47A

46-49   46-50

46-51

Cabot Tower:
Built 1897–1900 to commemorate the 400th anniversary of John Cabot's discovery of Newfoundland, it stands atop Signal Hill (Elevation 500 ft.), overlooking the entry to St. John's Harbour.

46-52

46-5

46-53

46-53A

46-5

walking distance of government offices at Confederation Building; Memorial University Campus; Institute of Fisheries and Marine Technology; the Fluvarium fronting on Long Pond; Arts and Culture Centre; Cabot Institute of Applied Arts and Technology; yet a wilderness-like quality is preserved within the park.

51. FLAT-TOPPED WHITE ASTER
(Aster umbellatus)
These white-rayed, terminal clusters are flat-topped as the name implies. Leaves are broad, lance-shaped, sessile, plentiful and straight-edged. Those pictured vary in height from 2–5 ft. and were growing in late-August in the floodplain of Seal Cove River, Conception Bay.

52. PURPLE-STEMMED ASTER
(Aster puniceus)
Numerous mauve to pale-purple rayed flowerheads in long-stalked panicles from sturdy, usually deep purple, stems up to 6 ft. high. Large, lance-shaped leaves alternate up the stem and may or may not be toothed. Those shown were growing in September beside Rennies River, St. John's and were photographed from the bridge on Elizabeth Avenue. These and a wide variety of other wildflowers in season populate the banks of the river and make the Quidi Vidi Walking Trail a pleasant, colourful and picturesque experience.

53. ROUGH-LEAVED ASTER
(Aster radula)
Pale-pink to mauve ray florets in few-flowered, long-stalked clusters terminating a 1–3 ft. stem. Bracts forming the involucre under the flowerhead tend to be recurved. Leaves are lance-shaped, finely toothed, alternating, sessile or slightly clasping the stem. The example shown was growing in late-August in the floodplain of Seal Cove River, Conception Bay.

53A.
A somewhat different form of A. radula was found growing in late-August in the Hawk Hills, inland from Holyrood at the southern extremity of Conception Bay, at an elevation of 500 ft. in an exposed, barren environment quite different from that of the previous example. Not much more than 1 ft. high, it has stalkless or very short-stalked flowerheads. It is probably Var. strictus. In the background are prostrate branches of Newfoundland Dwarf Birch (Betula michauxii), recognized by its coarsely-toothed, fan-shaped leaves.

54. SLENDER ASTER
(Aster gracilis)
Pink-rayed flowerheads in a terminal, long-stalked, few-flowered panicle. Its wiry, unbranched stem is usually not more than 1 ft. tall. Leaves are lance-shaped, sessile and untoothed. Note the acute junction of stem leaves and the 1 or 2 leaf-like bracts on the flower stalks. However, the example shown has 20–30 ray florets rather then the 9–12 described in Gray's Manual.

On our first visit to Indian Arm Pond we canoed out beyond the islands and across to the opposite side, pausing on the way to follow and observe a pair of loons with their one chick. We could not venture close to them, partly because we did not want to disturb them and partly because, within a certain distance, the dogs tensed and prepared to leap from the canoe in pursuit. Surprisingly, such instances have not overturned us yet, but there is always a possible first time to be considered. We always wear life-jackets so loss of equipment rather then hazard to life was a concern. When we eventually arrived on the far shore we found these pretty pink asters growing up between the rocks.

55. BOG ASTER
(Aster nemoralis)
These pale purple, short, single-flowerhead, narrow-leaved asters are commonly found on

marshes from the end of July onwards. This one was growing on a marsh near Seal Cove in Conception Bay. Note the numerous, narrow, unstalked (sessile) leaves with edges tending to turn under (revolute) and the sparsity of leaves on the uppermost portion of the stem.

56. NEW YORK ASTER
(Aster novae-belgii)
This aster is widespread throughout the Island portion of the Province. It is very adaptable to different environments, but in doing so it assumes a variety of forms which at times may not be easily recognized. The typical form has stalked, mauve-rayed flowerheads (about 30 rays per head) arising from axils of the upper leaves. The stem is leafy, smooth, unbranched, and may be 1–3 ft. high. Leaves are long, narrow, straight-edged or slightly toothed, sessile to clasping, and alternate spirally up the stem. The example shown was growing in late-September beside Topsail Highway, near the Town Hall in Paradise.

56A.
This is the form which *Aster novae-belgii* takes when growing in wetland conditions. Note the lance-shaped, untoothed leaves bunched around the upper half of the stalk as though the plant is holding its skirt up from the dampness below. Flowerheads have about 30 narrow ray florets. The plant may grow to 3 ft.

56B.
A carpet of these pink to pale-pink asters, none over 1 ft. high were a colourful display one sunny Sunday morning in September. The leaves are those of *Aster novi-belgii* and a few of the flowerheads have 30 rays, but most have 12–20 rays. These were growing beside Thorburn Road, St. John's.

57. NEW ENGLAND ASTER
(Aster novae-angliae)
Relatively long, narrow, violet-purple ray-florets (40–50) extending from the central disc of yellow tube-florets. Long, sharp-pointed, lance-shaped, untoothed, strongly clasping leaves are crowded along a tall, branching stem. Flowerheads occur in clusters at the tip of branches. The example shown was growing at Jack's Pond Camping Park in late-July.

58. BEGGAR-TICKS/STICK-TIGHT
(Bidens frondosa)
Older sections of cities are often rife with wildflowers growing in little secluded places and from cracks and spaces between concrete and stone where they are protected from the elements and warmed by the energy absorbing and reflective qualities of the urban environment. Beggar-ticks are a common occurrance here. They differ from other flowers of the Composite Family in that the bracts surrounding the flowerhead are long, leaf-green and look like green-petalled flowers. Flowerheads have no ray florets. Note also the wide, three-part, strongly toothed leaves. These were growing in a mud hole alongside Portugal Cove Road where it passes Windsor Lake, a source of water supply for St. John's. The picture was taken in mid-September, more than a month later than those growing in downtown St. John's. The name "stick-tight" refers to its barbed seed case, designed to stick to animal fur, and thus being transported to new or distant locations.

59. JOE-PYE WEED
(Eupatorium maculatum)
This is commonly seen along river banks from mid-August onwards, but more frequently as thickly growing concentrations, rather than singly as shown here. Having parked our camper on the site of an old saw-mill at the end of the narrow gravel road to Lady Pond, north of Smith's Sound, Trinity Bay, we walked about a mile along a logging trail which led to another old saw-mill site. The water was shallow here and protected by several islands with a wide expanse of level fore-shore on which iris, joe-pye weed, and small clumps of alders were the main

68

46-56   46-56A   46-57

46-56B

City Hall, St. John's:
Built 1970 on the north side of New Gower Street in
downtown St. John's. The billboard to the left marks this as
Mile 0 of the Trans-Canada Highway.

46-58

46-59

46-60

46-60A

Communications:
Increasing use of satellite and fiber optic transmission systems may eventually negate the need for tower concentrations on strategic elevations, such as shown here atop the Hawk Hills, near Holyrood, Conception Bay.

46-60B

46-61

46-62

growth. Unfortunately the wind was such during the several days we spent here that we could not safely use the canoe to explore the remaining perimeter of the pond.

60. MANY-RAYED GOLDENROD
(*Solidago multiradiata*)
Tightly packed corymb-like clusters of yellow flowerheads terminating stout, reddish, solitary stems seldom exceeding 1 ft. high. Long-stalked subsidary clusters arise from axils of the upper leaves. Stem leaves are sessile to clasping, long lance-shaped and with untoothed margins. Basal leaves may be more spatulate in shape, short stalked and have finely toothed margins. The example shown was growing in mid-July at Point Riche on the west coast of the Great Northern Peninsula. Note that the upper portion of the stem is somewhat whitened.

60A.
Young budding spherical clusters of many-rayed goldenrod atop thick, reddish, 4–6 inch, hairy stem. Basal and clasping stem leaves are lance-shaped, slightly hairy and finely toothed. These were growing at Watt's Point Calcareous Barrens in mid-July.

60B.
This example was also growing at Watt's Point at the same time as A. In overall appearance it looks somewhat like Arrow-leaved Sweet Coltsfoot (*Petasites sagittatus*) – note the leaf-like bracts subtending the flowerheads; triangular, sheathing stem leaves; and the larger leaf lying along the ground at the foot of the stem. However, we can find no record of any of the genus *Petasites* with yellow flowerheads. We therefore conclude that this is a form of *S. multiradiata*.
The variety and complexity of low growth covering the "Crowberry Lawns" of Watt's Point Calcareous Barrens is epitomized in this photograph by the Crowberry

(*Empetrum eamesii*), two types of willow leaves (the round dark-green leaf is *Salix reticulata* and the elliptical light-green leaf is *Salix calcicola*), and the natal flower spike of I know not what receiving womb-like protection from its leaf.

Life is so fragile, yet so strong and free!
Our roots hold the mystery of what we may be.
Through ages eternal we change with the times,
Adapting and thriving in various climes.
Each generation has problems unique,
Which tend to divide the strong from the weak.
Survivors have stored in their memory chain
The means of surviving these things once again.
We know not the why or the where of the strong,
But the deep-rooted life
of the world moves along.

61. ALPINE GOLDENROD
(*Solidago cutleri*)
A short, compact, smooth stemmed goldenrod not more than a foot high. Flowerheads are in a dense terminal raceme. Basal leaves are relatively long, spatulate to lance-shaped, finely to coarsely toothed, and with purplish leaf stalks. Stem leaves are similar but sessile; clasp the stem and arch outwards. The example shown was growing in late-August on the barrens atop the Hawk Hills, several miles inland from Holyrood at the head of Conception Bay.

62. PURSH'S GOLDENROD
(*Solidago purshii*)
This is also a relatively short goldenrod, seldom exceeding 2 ft. in height. Note its smooth wine-red stem; narrow lance-shaped, untoothed, sessile or very short stalked stem leaves, and its longer, spatulate lower leaves. Its yellow goldenrod flowerheads are in a tight, bulbous, branching terminal raceme. Many of these were growing singly and well separated from each other throughout a mossy barrens area in Jack's Pond Camping Park in late-August.

As with other members of the Goldenrod genus, it is rather difficult to visually distinguish between closely similar species because of the extent of variability to which some of these species are prone.

63. ROUGH-STEMMED GOLDENROD
(*Solidago rugosa*)

"Rough-stemmed" refers to the hairiness of the main stem. But this is not very helpful in recognition as others, such as Canada Goldenrod (*Solidago canadensis*), are similarly hairy along the upper stem. However, the leaves are broader and feather-veined rather than 3-nerved as in Canada Goldenrod. Flowerheads have 6–10 ray florets and the flower racemes are commonly confined to the outer portion of branches, thus presenting an elm-shaped appearance, although many variations occur as a result of hybridization.

In late-August we parked our camper in a small clearing at Rhodies Pond along the old railway branch-line to Placentia. Only three cars passed our site during the three days we were there. The solitude was a spiritually refreshing experience. Particularly memorable was the early morning stillness, mist rising in wisps from the pond, and the occasional plaintive calls from a family of loons constantly fishing up and down the length of the pond. On one occasion we met a young male moose on the roadway.

63A.

An example of the variability of *Solidago rugosa*. Note the more plume-like appearance and the occurrence of leaf-like bracts throughout the flower racemes. This colourful mass of flowers turned an average Sunday afternoon walk in mid-August into a beautifully memorable occasion. They were growing a little way west of the Fluvarium on Long Pond - an attractively styled, three-level, octagonal building, primarily designed to display and monitor the underwater habi-

tat of the Rennie's River-Long Pond System. The system supports domiciled Brook Trout and a large seasonal run of Brown Trout. An attempt is being made to reintroduce Atlantic Salmon. The river system had been seriously degraded by urbanizing influences from the mid-1800's onwards, but is now substantially in process of revitalization.

64. ELLIOTT'S GOLDENROD
(*Solidago elliottii*)

A smooth stem with crowded, elliptical, short-pointed leaves of constant size along the length of the stem. Flower racemes are divergent and occur only on the top-most portion of the stem. (This species is not recorded by Rouleau as being present in Newfoundland. It is possible, therefore, that it may be a local hybrid, recognizing that goldenrod are quite prone to hybridization.) The example shown was growing profusely along the edge of the roadway entrance to La Manche Camping Park in mid-September. Most Provincial Parks close for the season after Labour Day, but continue to be pleasant locations, particularly in their new-found solitude, for sunny walks in the country. The colourfully marked butterfly was one of many of the same type fluttering among the goldenrod on this occasion.

65. BOG GOLDENROD
(*solidago uliginosa*)

A tall, wand-like solitary form of goldenrod, usually found standing like sentinels in marshy locations. Note the firm, straight, dark red stem with a narrow, bulbous terminal raceme of numerous small flowerheads. Small, lance-shaped, sessile, untoothed leaves alternate along the stem, with vestigial racemes also occurring in the axils of the upper leaves. Basal leaves are larger and longer (about a foot long), untoothed and clasp the stem. This specimen was more than 5 ft. high, growing in marshy land along the shoreline of Indian Arm Pond. A pitcher plant and several bog

46-63

46-63A

The Fluvarium:
Located in Pippy Park,
St. John's, on the north
bank of Long Pond.

46-64

46-65

46-65A   *46-66*   *46-67*

46-68

Cold Ocean Research Centre:

A National Research Council facility within Memorial University's campus, conducts research in nautical design and ocean phenomena.

46-69

asters were growing alongside. To the rear is an alder bush and also a northeastern rose which has finished flowering and is in process of forming its rosehip seed packages.

65A.
Bog Goldenrod's variability in size is shown by this example, no more than 6 inches high, growing at Powles Point, Trepassey in early-August.

66. LARGE-LEAVED GOLDENROD
(*Solidago macrophylla*)
The flower of this goldenrod is larger than most of the preceding ones. Its basal leaves are large, pointed-ovate, stalked and coarsely toothed. Stem leaves are also ovate but smaller, short stalked to sessile, and may or may not be toothed. Stalked flowerheads arise from the axils of the upper leaves. This specimen was growing in mid-August at the edge of a clearing recently occupied by a sawmill alongside the roadway to Lady Pond, north of Smith Sound, Trinity Bay.

67. SEASIDE GOLDENROD
(*Solidago sempervirens*)
Stalked clusters of fairly large flowers terminate a stout, unbranched, smooth, brownish-red stem. Leaves are long-elliptical, untoothed, and sessile or slightly clasp the stem. The example shown was about 2 ft. high growing in late-August in a small marshy depression on the Hawk Hills, 2–3 miles inland from Holyrood, Conception Bay. The Pitcher Plant (*Sarracenia purpuria*) in the lower left corner of the photograph, the Dwarf Birch (*Betula michauxii*), and the Rough-leaved Aster (*Aster radula*) are typical of this type of environment.

68. LANCE-LEAVED GOLDENROD
(*Solidago graminifolia*)
This goldenrod seldom exceeds 3 ft. in height in Newfoundland but may be taller elsewhere. It has narrow 2–4 nerved, grass-like,

sessile, untoothed leaves and flowerheads in a flat or slightly rounded terminal umbel. The example shown was growing profusely in mid-September at the western end of Long Pond, to the rear of the Cold Ocean Research Building on MUN Campus. This building is quite extensive, containing several large tanks in which water current, wave action and ice formation may be simulated for practical research in nautical design and ocean phenomena.

It would appear that the butterfly seen in the photograph followed us from La Manche where it was enjoying Elliott's Goldenrod (#64). However, it is more likely that this type of butterfly is symbiotically associated with goldenrod flowers.

69. SLENDER FRAGRANT GOLDENROD
(*Solidago tenuifolia*)
Similar to Lance-Leaved Goldenrod (*S. graminifolia*), but has finer, narrower leaves with a single nerve or vein along the middle of the leaf rather than several parallel veins as in *S. graminifolia*. Note also that the flower umbels terminating each branch from the main stem all rise to the same height, giving an overall flat-topped appearance. The example shown was growing in mid-September in a fallow section of the Anglican Cemetery on Kenmount Road.

This cemetery has a pleasant aspect from the highway. The roadway entry curves around a small, grass-banked pond to cross a little stream. It is located on high ground overlooking the City of Mount Pearl. A lack of tree, bush or hedge planting gives the site a rather bleak and barren appearance. This contrasts strongly with the older Anglican Cemetery beside Quidi Vidi Lake in downtown St. John's. It is sited on low-lying, park-like land, graced with many mature trees, and is well protected from prevailing winds.

70. MUGWORT
(*Artemesia vulgaris*)

A tall, slim plant, up to 5 ft. in height, usually growing in fairly thick groups. Its sturdy straight stem is dark red and bears many deeply cleft and sharply pointed leaves which are dark green above and downy-white beneath. Spikes of small reddish-brown flowerheads arise from leaf axils. The example shown was growing in mid-August near the Health Sciences Centre off Prince Philip Parkway, St. John's.

71. WHITE MUGWORT
(*Artemesia lactiflora*)

This tall, stately weed was rising ghost-like in late-July among a patch of burdock leaves in a run-down vacant lot at the west end of Water Street in St. John's, although it would appear from the background that this was quite a rural location. Flowers are white disc florets in long racemes arching from the upper leaf axils of an erect reddish stem up to 5 ft. high. Leaves are compound, deeply lobed, sessile and whitened with fine hairs on the underside.

72. ABSINTH WORMWOOD
(*Artemesia absinthium*)

The stem, leaves and flowerhead involucre are all white-downy in appearance. Small drooping flowerheads of greenish-yellow disc florets occur in loose, ascending racemes from leaf axils along most of the 2–3 ft. stem. Leaves are pinnate, deeply lobed, sessile, whitened on both sides, and lobes are rounded rather than pointed. The example shown was growing in early-August in the farming community of Lethbridge, Bonavista Bay, where we had gone with a group to demonstrate square dancing at their 2-day Farmer's Field Day. A wonderful time was had by all.

Changing Seasons at Long Pond, St. John's:

Spring

Early Summer

46-70

Late Summer

46-71

Fall

46-72

47-1

Terra Nova National Park:
Resting at the end of a portage near
Pitt's Pond.

48-1

Cow Head:
A narrow neck of land connects Cow Head with the
mainland where the Town of Cow Head extends along the
shoreline. Blue in the distance rise the Long Range
Mountains.

49-1

Monocotyledons

47. WATER PLANTAIN FAMILY
(Alismataceae)

Aquatic plants usually found in sheltered recesses of shallow, muddy-bottomed, freshwater ponds. Flowers have 3 broad petals (usually white), 3 sepals, 6 stamens, and a superior ovary consisting of a central multitude of carpels. Leaves are parallel-veined, varying in shape among species from oval to arrow-shaped, to narrow and grass-like. Rouleau's List records only three members of the family occurring in the province: 1 of the genus *Alisma* (water plantain) and 2 of the genus *Sagittaria* (arrowhead).

1. GRASS-LEAVED ARROWHEAD
(Sagittaria graminea)

White 3-petalled flowers usually in stalked whorls of three at the extremity of single, unbranched stems rising from a basal whorl of grass-like, parallel-veined leaves. The example shown was growing in mid-August among the rocks in a small mud-plain at the edge of Pitt's Pond, a provincial reserve adja-cent to Terra Nova National Park. It was a bright, cloudless day and we had canoed across Pitts Pond with our dogs, keeping well out from shore so they would not be tempt-ed to jump out to chase shore-birds. At one point we stopped in at a cabin located in a sheltered, sandy-bottomed portion of the pond and added our names to a visitor's book left as an item of interest for passers-by.

48. ARROW-GRASS FAMILY
(Juncaginaceae)

A small family of plantain-like plants having a long spike of small flowers and usually occurring in coastal marshes.

1. MARINE ARROW-GRASS
(Triglochin maritimum)

Tiny, short-stalked, white-petalled flowers in a long narrow spike atop a leafless stem up to 2 ft. or more high. A rosette of long, narrow, grass-like leaves arise from the root. The example shown was growing in mid-July in a marsh near the camping park at Cow Head, Gros Morne National Park.

49. LILY FAMILY
(Liliaceae)

The typical flower is bell-shaped with 3 petals and 3 sepals (petals and sepals often being indistinguishable), 6-stamens and a single pistil. Leaves are parallel veined except in the Trillium genus where the longitudinal veins are also branched.

1. WILD LILY-OF-THE-VALLEY/ CANADA MAYFLOWER
(Maianthemum canadense)

A single terminal raceme of stalked pairs of white, flowers atop a slender 3-6 inch stem. 4 Stamens project laterally from the base of 4 sharply recurved petals. It is unclear whether or not these petals represent 2 sepals and 2 petals. There are usually 2 heart-shaped, alternate, sessile leaves on the stem. The specimen shown was pho-tographed at Indian Arm Pond in early July.

2. STARRY FALSE SOLOMON'S-SEAL
(*Smilacina stellata*)
A single, terminal raceme of white starry flowers atop a sturdy 6-10 inch stem having large, elliptical, clasping, closely spaced, alternate, leaves. Those shown were grow-ing in a bog beside the Trans-Canada Highway west of Gander in early-July.

2A.
A much smaller plant (3–4 inches high), sim-ilar to or a stunted version of *S. stellata*, found growing near Stephenville in mid-June, has only two flowers and its leaves are round and saucer-shaped.

3. THREE-LEAVED FALSE SOLOMON'S SEAL
(*Smilacina trifolia*)
Similar to *S. stellata* but smaller; flowers fewer and more widely spaced; its 3 broad elliptical leaves clasp and sheath the stem. These were also growing in the bog west of Gander at the same time as the example shown for *S. stellata*.

4. CLINTONIA/BLUE-BEAD LILY/ CORN LILY
(*Clintonia borealis*)
Up to 6 greenish-yellow bell-shaped flowers atop a straight, leafless stalk. Basal leaves (usually 3) are broad-elliptical and parallel veined. The specimen shown was growing at Aspen Brook, west of Grand Falls, in mid-June. A rather spectacular waterfall is locat-ed just north of the highway at Aspen Brook. The resulting "pothole" or chasm and down-stream freshwater beach provide a natural swimming pool environment, particularly attractive to the younger generation.

5. TWISTED-STALK/WHITE MANDARIN
(*Streptopus amplexifolius*)

A long, sinuous, smooth stem with pointed-oval, alternate, clasping leaves. Single or paired greenish-white flowers with deeply recurved sepals and petals hang from leaf axils on long flower stalks beneath each leaf. These were found growing in a damp, well shaded depression along a trail at Salton's Brook in Terra Nova National Park in mid-July. It was a warm, humid, overcast day and we had worn our ponchos because of intermittent rain showers. The trail took us through a variety of terrain and forest types. Of particular interest was a section of trail passing alongside a beaver dam where the walkway was constructed at a level where-by the observer was almost eyeball to eye-ball with the beavers, who did not seem to be overly concerned about our presence.

6. ROSE TWISTED-STALK
(*Streptopus roseus*)
Similar to *S. amplexifolius* but with pink to purple bell-shaped flowers having only the tips of the petals recurved. Note also that the stem is reddish and slightly hairy. These were growing at Watt's Point Calcareous Barrens in mid-July together with *S. amplexifolius*. This and the previous photo-graph were taken two years apart. Seasonal variation may therefore account for their flowering at the same time of year in quite different climatic locations. These were grow-ing in Cow Parsnip snow beds exposed to on-shore westerly winds from the Straits of Belle Isle. Others were found flowering at the same time in sheltered locations beneath stands of "tuckamore" (patches of wind-stunted but thickly growing coniferous trees almost impervious to the elements) at a high-er elevation farther back from the coastline.

7. NORTHERN ASPHODEL
(*Tofieldia pusilla*)
Greenish-white, 6-petalled flowers growing in a short, compact spike atop a slender, 6-inch, leafless stem. Short, lance-shaped, lin-ear leaves arise from the roots forming a mat at the base of the flower stems. The clump of

49-2

49-2A

49-3

49-6

49-4

49-5

49-7

49-9

49-8

50-1B

50-1A

Barachois Camping Park:
Veronica, iris, yellow and orange hawkweed – all looking fresh as dasies – were blooming at the time. (see 46-24, p.61)

50-2

flowers shown was growing at Watt's Point Calcareous Barrens in mid-July.

8. ROMAN HYACINTH
(*Hyacinthus orientalus albulus*)
This Hyacinth occurs only in white. It differs from commercial Dutch Hybrids in that several stems arise from a single bulb and its flower spikes have fewer flowers. The example shown was growing in mid-June in a naturalized section of Bowring Park. It is included here because this section of the park has remained in a naturalized state since the park was established.

9. NODDING TRILLIUM
(*Trillium cernuum*)
A whorl of 3 broad, pointed-oval wavy-edged, branch-veined leaves terminating a sturdy, erect, smooth unbranched, otherwise leafless stem up to 18 inches high. A single flower having 3 green sepals and 3 white petals arises from the centre of the whorl of leaves but the flower stalk turns immediately downwards between leaf axils so that the flower opens beneath the leaf umbrella. Hence the name – "Nodding" Trillium. The anthers of its 6 stamens are pink. The example shown was growing along with many others among alder bushes in a marshy location beside the James Callahan Trail, Gros Morne National Park, in early-June.

50. IRIS FAMILY
(*Iridaceae*)
These are 3-part, bilaterally symmetrical flowers in which the sepals may be similar to or the same as the petals. Flower buds are encased in leaf-like bracts which form a protective shield or "spathe" around the base of the flower. Leaves are long, flattened and parallel-veined.

1. BLUE FLAG
(*Iris versicolor*)
Blue-violet flowers in few-flowered, long-stalked (up to 3 ft.), terminal clusters arising from overlapping, sword-shaped, sheathing leaves. The 3 sepals ("falls") are large, spatulate, arched downward, blue or purple on the outer edge, deeply-veined throughout, white in the centre and towards the base, sometimes suffused with yellow. The 3 petals ("standards") are upright, smaller than the sepals and alternate with them. From the centre of the flower 3 broad petal-like styles ("crest") arise and arch over the sepals (through the space between petals). This 3-part style or "crest" has an upturned serrated outer edge (claw) and covers the stamens projecting between the petals. Two photographs are shown:

1A.
Side view, showing leaves, bract-enclosed buds, and the vertical nature of the "standards".

1B.
An overhead view showing the flower parts. Both were taken in early-July at Barachois Camping Park on the Trans-Canada Highway near Stephenville, just north of the road junction to Burgeo.

2. YELLOW IRIS
(*Iris pseudacorus*)
Flowers having the same form as Blue Flag but all of its parts (falls, standards, crest and claw) a sunny yellow colour with sturdy green stems rising to 3 ft. or more. Sword-shaped basal leaves (1 or 2) rise to the height of the stem and have a prominent and more or less central ridge running along the length of the leaf. The example shown is one of an

extensive mass growing in a wet swale beside the roadway near Flatbay, on the west coast of the Island, south of Stephenville, in mid-July. A similarly extensive, but separate, mass of Blue Flag was flowering in the swale at the same time.

3. BLUE-EYED GRASS
(*Sisyrinchium bermudianum*)
Small blue to purple flowers on 6–12 inch grass-like stems, usually found growing in tufts. The 3 petals and 3 sepals are alike, giving the appearance of a 6-petalled flower. Note the deeper coloured parallel veining and the small pointed tip at the end of each petal and sepal. A single flower projects from the end of each grass-like stem on a

short, round flower stalk backed by a spathe-like bract rising above the flower. The example shown was growing in a drainage swale leading to the shoreline at Marystown in early-July. Some of the flowers have matured to seed formation showing the spathe more clearly. Note also that the bright-yellow pistil projects out of the flower tube and is surmounted by a six-pointed stigma, the points drooping downward along the style. Three pairs of stamens are contained within the flower tube. The drooping stigma points usually indicate that cross-pollination has not been achieved and the stigma in this way is stretching towards the pollen of its own anthers to achieve self-pollination.

51. ORCHID FAMILY
(*Orchidaceae*)
Orchids are quite varied in flower form. The flower parts arise above the ovary and are comprised of 3 sepals, which may be petal-like, and 3 petals, one of which is usually markedly different from the others – being widened, elongated or otherwise formed into a "lip" or a "sac" – and may also be prolonged behind as a "spur". Leaves are undivided (simple), straight-edged, parallel-veined, clasp the stem, and vary in size from scale-like to quite large. Orchid species found in northern climates are all "terrestrial" (having a root system drawing sustenance from the soil), whereas many tropical species are "epiphytic" (having a root system capable of drawing sustenance from the air and thus flourishing above the ground in tree branches).

1. ONE LEAF ORCHIS/ SMALL ROUND- LEAVED ORCHIS
(*Orchis rotundifolia*)
(May also be found listed under the genus name "*Amerorchis*"). A 4–6 inch stem bearing a terminal cluster of pale-pink and purple flowers. Its single basal leaf is large and oval. Each flower has 3 petals backed by 3 sepals. The 2 upper petals are purple and form a hood above the opening to the yellow stamens and stigma. The lower petal is a broad, 4-lobed, pale-pink lip with purple spots. The 3 sepals are pale-pink. The 2 lower sepals droop to either side of the lip. The upper sepal is broader than the others and arches forward forming a canopy above the purple hood formed by the two upper

petals. The specimen shown was growing in mid-July at Watt's Point Calcareous Barrens. Note the density and variety of background growth typical of the Calcareous Barrens, which here includes shiny willow-leaves (*Salix spp.*) and a pair of pink, urn-shaped flowers of Teaberry (*Gaultheria procumbens*).

2. WHITE FRINGED ORCHID
(*Habenaria blephariglottis*)
A raceme of white flowers having outwardly projecting, beard-like, fringed lips and long, inward pointing spurs, on a stem seldom exceeding 10 inches in overall height. Clasping, sharply-pointed leaves of diminishing length (only the uppermost one is seen in the photograph) alternate up the stalk.

76

L'Anse Aux Meadows:
The author standing between a reconstructed Viking community sod house and a replica of a Viking boat, displayed at the L'Anse Aux Meadows World Heritage Site, at the extreme tip of the Great Northern Peninsula where Vikings wintered about the year 1000 A.D.

50-3

51-1

Tuckamore:
An example of windswept, low-growing spruce and fir trees commonly occurring along the coastline north of Gros Morne National Park. (see 49-6, p.74)

51-2

51-3

51-4

51-5

51-6

Western Brook Pond:
Mist-shrouded cliffs rise 2,000 ft. above the edge of
Western Brook Pond.

**Indian Head Park,
Stephenville:**
The airport and buildings of
Ernest Harmon Air Force
Base, now converted to
civilian use, is the backdrop
for players on the municipal
golf course at Stephenville.

The example shown was growing in a marsh near the intake to the penstock carrying water to Newfoundland Power's hydro-electric generating plant at Seal Cove, Conception Bay.

This Generating Plant was built in the early 1920's by United Towns Electric Company (Inc. 1902 to provide service to Heart's Content, Carbonear and Harbour Grace, later extending this to all the Avalon Peninsula except St. John's). This company, together with other electric utilities, amalgamated with Newfoundland Light and Power Company in 1966, recently renamed Newfoundland Power.

3. RAGGED FRINGED ORCHID
(*Habenaria lacera*)

To call this orchid "ragged"
does not really treat it right.
It diminishes the angel host,
dressed all in white,
Dancing round the flower tip,
happy as can be,
They've dressed for the occasion,
as anyone can see.
Let's call it "angel orchid"
to give it more acclaim.
H. angelica-fimbriata
can be its Latin name.

Similar in its whiteness, height and general appearance to the White Fringed Orchid, its sepals and upper two petals are smaller. Its lip, about the same size as *H. blephariglottis*, is divided into three parts, each part having fringed edges made up of long filaments. [This flower looks very much like Prairie White Fringed Orchid (*H. leucophaea*) which occurs only in the Prairie Provinces.] The spur of the flower and the stem leaves are also similar in size, arrangement and location. The specimen shown was also growing in late-July in a marsh near Seal Cove Brook, the same time as the White Fringed Orchid.

4. SMALL PURPLE FRINGED ORCHID
(*Habenaria psycodes*)

The example shown is about 1 ft.high and is more pink than purple. The lipped petal is divided into three distinct parts with fringed edges, similar to *H. lacera*. However, the sepals and upper petals have a different configuration and the flower raceme is longer and more abundantly flowered. These were growing on a wet hillside near Flat Bay on the West Coast of the Province, south of Stepenville, in mid-July.

5. PURPLE FRINGELESS ORCHID
(*Habenaria peramoena*)

This flower is similar to *H. psycodes* except that the divisions of the lipped petal are not fringed or only very slightly so. Note also the pyramidal shape of the flower raceme and the large oval lowest leaves. This and others were growing at the same time and in the same general location as *H. psycodes*.

6. BOG CANDLE/LEAFY WHITE ORCHID
(*Habenaria dilatata*)

Commonly found in wet fields and roadside ditches in July, these orchids have a cylindrical spike of white flowers extending along the upper half of its thick strong stem, sometimes rising as high as 2 ft. overall. Leaves are long, linear and strongly clasp the stem in diminishing length upward from the base. The flowers have a slender, drooping unfringed lip, two lateral petals and a hood. A spur, about the same length as the lip, droops downward from the back of the flower. This particular specimen was found, along with many others, growing in a small boggy area at "The Arches", a scenic coastal site with picnicking accommodations located on the Great Northern Peninsula a little way north of the north boundary of Gros Morne National Park. Leafy White Orchid (*H. dilatata*) has a variety of other local names, of which "scent-bottle", "smell-smock" and "wild hyacinth" are but a few.

7. LITTLE CLUB-SPUR ORCHID
(*Habenaria clavellata*)

This little orchid is common to many marshes on the Avalon Peninsula and elsewhere in Newfoundland. "*Platanthera*" is an alternative genus name now substantially replaced by "*Habenaria*". Gray's Manual of Botany (edited by Fernald) points out that in Newfoundland *H. clavellata* is not as tall as elsewhere and as a result its leaves are broader; flowers in the raceme are fewer on average; together with several other differences which in total have been accepted as constituting a distinct variety – *Var. ophioglossoides* (meaning: somewhat like the fern *ophioglossum*).

With the foregoing as background, *H. clavellata* (*Var. ophioglossoides*) has a short raceme of 8–10 creamy-green flowers projecting more or less horizontally in all directions on stout flower stalks. Each flower is stubby and bud-like in appearance, the petals and lip not projecting beyond the sepals (at least in none of the specimens we have seen). A substantial spur, about three-times the flower length, extends backward along the flower stalk giving each flower a club-like appearance ("*clavellata*" means club shaped). Overall height seldom exceeds 1 ft. One or two lance-shaped leaves clasp the stem at its base and rise a quarter to a third of its height. A smaller bract-like leaf also clasps the stem about one-third the way up. Those shown were growing in late-July on a marsh near Seal Cove River, Conception Bay.

8. NORTHERN GREEN ORCHID
(*Habenaria hyperborea*)

A tightly crowded spike of greenish-white flowers atop a sturdy 1–2 ft. stem. Numerous overlapping lily-like leaves ascend and clasp the stem. Each flower arises from the base of a green bract. The blunt, downward projecting, whitish tongue is hooded by the upper two greenish petals. The wing-like sepals are also greenish and a short spur curves downwards to the rear. The examples shown were growing in mid-July on the height overlooking Mayfield Ballpark in Stephenville.

9. SMALL NORTHERN BOG ORCHID/ ONE-LEAF REIN-ORCHID
(*Habenaria obtusata*)

White to greenish-white flowers arise singly on short, well-spaced, alternating stalks along the upper half of the stem. A long narrow green lip projects conspicuously downward and a slender spur extends to the rear. A single broad leaf occurs at the base of the 1 ft. stem and there is a large leaf-like bract on the lower half of the stem. One such basal leaf may be seen in the lower right-hand corner of the picture. The group shown was growing in mid-July from the mossy ground cover of a mature fir and spruce forest surrounding Berry Hill Pond in Gros Morne National Park.

Berry Hill Pond is skirted by a nicely primitive walking trail. A notice at the boardwalk bridge crossing the outlet stream refers to the pond being one of only a few inhabited by Green Frogs. Up to the 1950's at least, Green Frogs were quite common in small ponds and marshes, but now have become quite noticeably scarce. Whether this is due to insecticides, acid rain, gap in the food chain, increased levels of ultra-violet radiation, or some other reason, is not known, but the Green Frog seems now to be a vanishing breed.

10. LARGE ROUND-LEAVED ORCHID
(*Habenaria orbiculata*)

This was also growing in mid-July near Berry Hill Pond, its flowers only in bud at this time; but the long spur, still in process of unfolding, can readily be seen. The two large, round basal leaves were 8–10 inches in diameter and the stem 2–2½ ft. high. Note the smaller lance-shaped bracts alternating along the stem and at each flower stalk.

51-7

51-8

51-9

Berry Hill Camping Park:
Our dog Kala, waiting for us to catch up, on a trail from the camping park to Berry Hill Pond.

51-10

51-11 *51-12* *51-12A*

51-13 *51-13A* *51-15*

51-14 *51-14A*

11. WHITE ADDER'S MOUTH
(*Malaxis brachypoda*)
(Sometimes: *M. monophyllos*). This too was growing near Berry Hill Pond in mid-July. At first glance it is like *H. obtusata*, except that there are more flowers more closely bunched along the upper stem; there is no spur; and the lip is short and heart shaped. (Quite different in fact, but only on closer inspection.)

12. GREEN ADDER'S MOUTH
(*Malaxis unifolia*)
A raceme of small, yellowish-green flowers atop a 4-inch stem rising from a single, ovate, embracing leaf. The example shown was growing in late-July in a marsh beside Seal Cove River, downstream from the Conception Bay Highway. Behind it can be seen the basal leaves of a Pitcher Plant (*Sarracenia purpurea*) poking up through the sphagnum moss.

12A.
Another form of Adder's Mouth, similar to *M. unifolia*, but quite different in its longer, narrower raceme, short flower stalks, and much larger leaf. Note the small white projections on each side of the central column (combined style and filaments). This was growing in mid-July at The Arches Picnic Park, north of Gros Morn National Park.

13. HOODED LADIES'-TRESSES
(*Spiranthes romanzoffiana*)
A triple-spiraled raceme of white flowers extending along the upper half of a 6–14 inch stem. Alternating, lily-like leaves clasp the stem and arch gracefully from it. Flowers project from the sturdy stem in close, orderly spirals. Wide, clasping, green bracts give the appearance of a collar around the base of each flower. The specimen shown was one of a substantial colony growing in mid-August in a drainage swale near the junction of the Burin Peninsula and Trans-Canada Highways.

13A.
This specimen of Hooded Ladies'-Tresses is included because it appears to be a slightly modified form. A dozen or so of these were growing on a steeply sloping grassy field in the Bond Estate Park at Whitbourne in mid-August. Each was growing in a location well separated from the others, and each one showed the initially horizontal stem growth and upward curving flower raceme characteristic of this specimen. None were over 6 inches tall.

14. YELLOW LADY'S SLIPPER
(*Cypripedium calceolus*)
A single flower on each stem. The most prominent feature is the much widened yellow lower petal shaped in the form of a slipper. The two brown upper lateral petals are elongated, and in this variety (*Var. parviflorum*) are spirally twisted. The three sepals are also brown. The upper one projects as a canopy above the slipper opening. The lower two assume a clasping position below the slipper. Basal leaves are wide, lance-shaped, have 5 distinct veins and clasp the stem. A single smaller leaf or bract rises from the stem immediately behind the flower. The example shown was growing at MUN Botanic Park in early June.

14A.
Var. planipetalum
Petals and sepals of this variety of Yellow Lady's Slipper (*C. calceolus*) are all yellow, and the lateral petals are not twisted. The example group shown was one of many growing at Point Riche on the Great Northern Peninsula in mid-July.

15. PINK LADY'S SLIPPER
(*Cypripedium acaule*)
The slipper of *C. acaule* is pink, clearly veined, drooping or pendent (more like a sac than a slipper) and does not have as large an opening into the sac as *C. calceolus*. Lateral petals and the 3 sepals have a purplish hue.

The leaf-like bract at the curvature of the stem forms a canopy over the flower, perhaps as a protective feature attractive to polinating insects and/or to prevent rain water from entering the sac. The stem is slightly downy (pubescent) and usually has three basal leaves of the type typical of the family. The photograph was taken in early-June at Indian Arm Pond, near the Lewisporte Road Junction.

16. SHOWY LADY'S SLIPPER
(Cypripedium reginae)

Behold, in regal red, the Queen!
Enthroned on lofty spires green
And crowned in purest white.

The royal court with banners gay
Proclaims itself along the way,
A rare and happy sight.

It represents a world serene;
A peak of nature's verdent scene;
A season at its height.

Let no molesting hand despoil
This fruit of mother nature's soil!
It reigns by godly right.

Several clumps of these were growing alongside the trail to Baker's Brook Falls in Gros Morne National Park in mid-July. How elegant and regal they looked, making the walk to the falls an even more pleasant and memorable occasion. The slipper is magenta, suffused with white beneath and to the rear. Lateral petals are pure white and not as elongate as in the Yellow and Pink Lady's Slippers. Its three sepals are also pure white and emphasize the slipper's rich colouration. The upper sepal is oval to round and projects forward forming a canopy over the slipper's opening. Large clasping strongly-veined oval leaves alternate up the stem and enfold it along its entire length. The bract behind the flower rises vertically from the stem.

17. ROSE POGONIA
(Pogonia ophioglossoides)

A single, large, dusty-rose-coloured flower atop a 6–12 inch stem having a broad, clasping leaf near its base and a smaller, bract-like leaf just below the flower. The flower has a distinctive, downward projecting, fringed and yellow-crested lip. Its upper two petals and the three sepals are the same colour and of similar pointed-oval shape. The specimen shown was growing in mid-August in a sphagnum marsh alongside Seal Cove River, Conception Bay.

18. CALOPOGON/GRASS PINK
(Calopogon tuberosus)

Grows to a foot or more high. Has one or two lance-shaped, sheathing, basal leaves and 4–5 pink to purple flowers 1–1½ inches across, blooming consecutively upwards along the stem. The spoon-shaped, filament-covered lip of the flower projects upwards, forming a canopy above a similarly shaped, outwardly extended column. Lateral petals are curved slightly backwards around their long axis. Sepals are the same colour as the petals. The example shown was growing in late-July in a sphagnum marsh alongside Seal Cove River (sometimes named *C. pulchellus*).

19. ARETHUSA/DRAGON'S MOUTH
(Arethusa bulbosa)

A single, pink (sometimes pale mauve) flower atop a 4–8 inch stem bearing 1–3 small scale-like bracts. A grasslike basal leaf develops after the flower matures and persists to the next season, enabling photosynthesis required for bulb regeneration. The down-curved lip of the flower is wider and longer than the other petals. It is wavy-edged, pink-spotted, suffused with white, and crested with many short, yellow to white filaments. Upper lateral petals curve forward forming a canopy above the lip. Petal-like sepals rise vertically behind the flower giving it a perky appearance. The photograph was taken in mid-July on a marsh near Stephenville.

Ten Mile Pond:
Viewed from atop
Gros Morne.

51-16

51-17   *51-18*   *51-19*

51-20   51-21   53

52-A   52-B

Young moose on a marsh:
Moose and peat marshes are
common occurrences
throughout the province.
Moose were introduced to the
Island in 1878 and again in
1904, and have since thrived
abundantly.

20. BOG TWAYBLADE
(*Liparis loeselii*)
A rather dishevelled looking little green orchid having a pair of relatively large, clasping basal leaves and a raceme of 6–12 yellowish-green flowers. The flower is comprised of a stubby projecting column; a short, trapezoidal-shaped lip; a pair of thread-like lateral petals; and three narrow sepals. The specimen shown was photographed on a marsh near Stephenville in mid-July.

21. SPOTTED CORALROOT
(*Corallorhiza maculata*)
The tallest of the Coralroot genus, its bare, 1 or 2 bracted, brownish-purple stem grows to a height of 1½ ft. and has a terminal raceme of similarly coloured flowers with a white, purple-spotted lip. Members of this orchid genus are entirely saprophytic, its rhizome resembling a piece of coral. The example shown was growing beside the James Callaghan Trail, Gros Morne National Park in mid-July.

52. PIPEWORT FAMILY
(*Eriocaulaceae*)
Members of this family occur in shallow water or along muddy shorelines. Most are restricted to tropical or temperate climates. Only one species, *Eriocaulon aquaticum*, is recorded in Rouleau's List of Newfoundland Plants. Its height is dependent on the normal depth of water in its natural surroundings, but is seldom more than 2 ft. high. The flowers are very small and white petalled, occurring in a single, dense, globular cluster atop a smooth, leafless, reed-like stem. Leaves are short, fleshy and sword-shaped, forming a mat around the base of the stem. Two examples are shown, both growing in mid-August.

52A.
Shows the flowerheads, stem and most of the basal leaves of plants growing along the shoreline of Southwest Pond, near Salmonier Line.

52B.
Shows the flowerheads and stems rising above the surface of the water where they were growing throughout a shallow inlet of Thorburn Lake.

53. CATTAIL FAMILY
(*Typhaceae*)
A small family of only 1 genus (*Typha*), of which Rouleau's List records only 1 species (*Typha latifolia*) in Newfoundland. Bullrush, as this species is commonly called, is the tallest member of the family, growing to 5 ft. or more in wet, marshy locations and usually in extensive colonies. It is a tall, slender, single-stemmed plant bearing its flowers in a tight, cylindrical, terminal raceme. The upper, narrower part of the raceme is comprised entirely of male flowers and extends downwards along the stem to meet the lower female portion. Once the male (staminate) raceme has produced its pollen, this portion dries up and is gradually blown away. The lower, female flowers, when pollinated, form a dark brown, cylindrical, fruiting body which persists well into winter. Leaves are very long, grass-like, clasp the stem and are strongly ascendant along it. The example shown was growing in mid-September in a highway ditch near Codroy, a farming community in the valley of the Codroy River, north of Port aux Basques.

54. BUR-REED FAMILY
(*Sparganiaceae*)

Aquatic and wetland plants having long thick, linear-veined, basal leaves in addition to similar, sessile stem leaves which may be more properly considered as bracts or stipules. Flowers are very small and occur in globular bur-like clusters on the stem. Lower and larger clusters are pistillate (female) flowers. The upper and smaller clusters are staminate (male) flowers. Plants may vary in height from 1–6 ft. or more, partly depending on water depth. Species are in some instances defined by the number of male or female clusters occurring on each stem. Rouleau's List of Newfoundland Plants includes only 1 genus – *Sparganium*, of which there are 9 recognized species. Two examples of *Sparganium* are shown as follows:

54A.
A short specimen, about 1 ft. high, growing at the edge of Southwest Pond on Salmonier Line in early-August. Note the long white stamen filaments with yellow anthers projecting from the upper clusters of male flowers, and pistils projecting from the single lower spherical female cluster.

54B.
Bur-reeds, also growing in early-August, in 2–3 ft. of water at Thorburn Lake, a provincial park alongside the Trans-Canada Highway about 20 miles south of Terra Nova National Park. Note the much longer leaves rising well above the flower stem and that there are 2 male clusters above 2 female clusters. A single female cluster, without an accompanying male cluster, may also be seen terminating a small branch rising from a leaf axil.

54-B

54-A

Twin Peaks:
Located northwards along
the highway from Port Aux
Basques, these are locally
called "Mae West Hills".

Port Aux Basques:
The ferry "Joseph and Clara
Smallwood" at Port Aux
Basques, loading for passage
to North Sydney, Nova
Scotia.

The Authors

Bill *(above), at the summit of Gros Morne, Gros Morne National Park, and June, (below) sitting with Kala in a backwater pool, when not hiking, canoeing and camping, enjoy modern square dancing. They raised five children and celebrated their 40th wedding anniversary in 1993.*

Glossary

Acute: being at a sharp angle (usually 30° or less) to the stem, leaf stalk or other reference.

Alternate: each leaf occurring on the opposite side of the stem in relation to the next leaf above and below it.

Angular: referring to the stem of a plant having corners, thus being square or multi-sided in cross-section, rather than round.

Anther: the portion of the stamen or male organ of the flower on which pollen is formed.

Apomictic: the ability of a plant to reproduce by apomixis.

Apomixis: the process or ability of a flower to form productive seed from female cells without requiring fertilization by pollen.

Ascending (Ascendant): the referenced portion or part of a plant having a distinct upward inclination or disposition.

Asexual: the process of vegetative plant reproduction by means of branching rootstock, the formation of bulbs, corms or tubers, or the lateral extension of runners.

Banner: uppermost petal of flowers of the Pea Family *(Leguminosae)*. Sometimes called "standard". See also "keel" and "wing".

Barb: a straight or curved, pointed outgrowth from a stem or stalk.

Barrens: exposed rocky or thin soil areas capable of supporting low and scrubby vegetation only.

Basal: at the base of the plant, usually referring to a location at or near the surface of the soil around the root of the plant.

Bearded: hair growth on one or more petals of a flower, commonly in relation to such occurrence in several species of violets.

Berry: a fleshy fruit containing several to numerous seeds, but commonly applied to any small fleshy fruit.

Bilateral symmetry: the construction of a flower such that if it was divided by a plane through its central axis, the two parts would be mirror images of each other.

Bract: a specialized protective scale-like leaf occurring at the base of a flower. It is neither a sepal nor a petal and may occur singly or in multiples.

Bristle: a stiff hair.

Bud: an undeveloped flower protected by sepals.

Bulb: the compact underground food storage and overwintering portion of some plants and includes the fleshy embryonic stem and leaves of the mature plant.

Bulbil: a small bulb-like growth, produced by some plants in leaf axils or in place of some flowers, capable of generating new growth.

Bushy: descriptive of leafy, multi-stemmed growth.

Calyx (Calyx tube): term applied to the sepals of a flower when considered as a group. Sepals may be separate or joined at the base. Where joined, a calyx tube is formed and the unjoined extremities are called the calyx lobes.

Cane: a term commonly applied to the woody stem of such plants as raspberries and roses.

Capsule: a type of seed container produced by some plants which splits open to release seeds when mature.

Carpel: one of the segments or cells which make up the ovary.

Caudex: the persistent base of an annual herbaceous stem.

Chlorophyll: the green pigment of plants which absorbs energy from light as needed to activate photosynthesis.

Clasping: descriptive of the form of the base of an unstalked leaf which folds or curves laterally around the stem of the plant.

Claw: a term specifically applied to the upturned, serrated extremity of the three petal-like styles of irises, but sometimes also applied to long, upturned petals of other flowers.

Cleistogamy: a process of self-pollination by production of flowers which do not open, but attain maturity while still enclosed by sepals.

Clump: a dense group of stems arising from the soil.

Cluster: flowers occurring in groups of few to many.

Column: in Orchids, a projecting organ combining the function of male filaments and the female style.

Compound: referring to leaves which consist of two or more leaflets arising from a single leaf stalk.

Corymb: a type of flower cluster in which flowers of the cluster occurring lower on the stem have longer stalks, resulting in a flat-topped appearance.

Creeping: a method of plant growth and proliferation by means of stems extending along the ground and rooting from nodes.

Crest: term applied to the horizontal portion of the petal-like style of irises which arch over the stamens.(see "claw")

Cross: a plant resulting from the cross-pollination of sub-species, rarely between species under natural conditions, and exhibiting characteristics of both parents.

Cross-pollination: the pollination of one plant by another, usually of the same species.

Cyme: a type of flower cluster in which flowers occur at the ends of branched, sometimes consecutively branched, flower stalks.

Dehisce: the release of seeds by splitting of the seed case.

Deltoid: a triangular shape.

Dicotyledon: the occurrence of two "seed-leaves" at the initial stage of plant growth (germination). This characteristic distinguishes between the two main groups of flowering plants.(See "monocotyledon")

Dioecious: the term applied to the characteristic of those species which bear male and female flowers on separate plants.

Disc: the round centre portion of the flowerhead occurring in some members of the Composite/Daisy Family consisting of a tightly packed arrangement of tubular florets.

Disc-floret: one of the many small tubular flowers in a "disc".

Dissected: descriptive of a leaf finely divided into narrow segments which may or may not be regular in shape.

Double-pinnate: a form of compound leaf having a branched mid-rib with leaflets arising from these branches.

(See: Pinnate - bi-pinnate)

Down (Downy): covered with soft hairs.

Drupe: a fleshy fruit usually containing a single seed encased by a hard protective layer or stone. Some berries are made up of many drupes or "druplets" as in raspberries and bake-apples.

Enzyme: a complex molecule (protein) produced to promote vital chemical reactions in the plant.

Erect: upright or vertical.

Falls: petal-like sepals which arch or droop downwards, usually in reference to irises.

Family: a unit of the plant classification system consisting of "genera" with similar or related characteristics. The latinized name usually ends in -aceae. "Families" with related characteristics are grouped as an "order" of the plant kingdom.

Fertilization (Cross-/Self-): the fusion of a pollen (male) cell with an ovule (female) cell to produce a viable seed. Cross-fertilization occurs as a result of pollination by pollen from another plant. Self-fertilization occurs as a result of pollination by pollen from the same flower or from a flower of the same plant.

Filament: the stalk bearing the pollen producing anther. The stalk and anther together comprise the stamen which is the male organ of a flower.

Fleshy: the characteristic of being thick or fattened due to prevalence of pulpy cells usually with a high water content.

Floret: one of the small flowers in a compound flowerhead, usually applied to those of the Composite/Daisy Family, but may sometimes be applied to flowers of the Pea Family, Parsley/Carrot Family and others.(See ray- and tube-floret)

Flower: the parts of a plant which contribute to or assist in reproduction through seed formation. This may include both male (stamens) and female (overy) parts as well as protective structures such as sepals and petals which may also be designed to attract pollinators. The simplest flower may have male or female parts only and a few protective scales.

Flowerhead: dense arrangement of florets.

Foliate (Foliage): having leaves.

Follicle: a seed case that splits along one side and contains a single seed.

Fringe: thread-like edging, usually of a petal.

Fruit: mature seed or seeds as may occur in a variety of forms, but most commonly referring to seeds encased in a pulpy and juicy matrix.

Fungus: a type of plant that reproduces by spores rather than seeds. Lacking chlorophyll it does not produce food by photosynthesis, but depends on other organisms for food.

Fused: two or more units joined or partly joined into a single unit, here usually referring to petals or sepals.

Genus (Pl.- Genera): a unit of the plant classification system consisting of "species" with similar or related characteristics. In the latinized naming system, the first name is the genus name and the second is the species name. Genera with similar characteristics are grouped as a "family".

Glandular: the characteristic of secreting oily, sticky or other substances through specialized cells.

Where such substances are secreted through hairs, these are called "glandular hairs".

Glomerule: a term sometimes applied to a tight cluster of small flowers.

Gynodioecious: the term applied to plants which may bear male and female flowers either on seperate plants or on the same plant.

Hairs: small, slender, unicellular or multicellular, protective outgrowths which may occur thickly or thinly in various locations on a plant.

Hastate: spear-shaped.

Hemiparasite: a plant which is only partly parasitic, such as some members of the Snapdragon Family, which tap into roots of neighbouring plants for water and minerals but are capable of producing their own sugars by photosynthesis.

Herb (Herbaceous): plants having soft, flexible, non-woody stems which die back at the end of each growing season.

Hermaphrodite: a flower which has both male and female reproductive parts.

Heterostylous: term applied to flowers of the same species which have more than one normal arrangement of stamens and styles. (eg. Purple Loosestrife)

Hood: descriptive of an enlarged upper petal projecting above the sexual parts of a flower. (eg. flowers of the Mint Family; some orchids; and Monkshood of the Buttercup Family.)

Hybrid (Hybridize): the offspring of two plants of different species or varieties of a species, exhibiting characteristics of both parents.

Insectivorous: descriptive of plants capable of trapping and digesting insects for food.

Interrupted: descriptive of flowers being irregularly spaced or grouped along the flower stem.

Involucre: a ring or overlapping series of rings of bracts occurring at the base of a flower cluster, most commonly occurring in the Composite/Daisy Family.

Irregular: descriptive of flowers which are neither radially nor axially symmetrical in overall appearance.

Keel: descriptive of the two lower petals of flowers of the Pea Family which are joined together lengthwise in the shape of a boat's hull to conceal the male and female parts.

Lanceolate: descriptive of the shape of a leaf being like that of the head of a lance or spear, rounded on the sides and graduating to a sharp tip.

Leaf: an outgrowth from the stem, branch or root of a plant. Varying greatly in size, shape and form among species, its usual purpose is to provide the specialized cell surface area necessary for plants to breath and photosynthesize. In some parasitic or saprophytic plants the leaf form may be small and vestigial, serving no apparant use in the plant's evolved state.

Leaf-axil: the angle formed by the junction of a leaf or leaf-stalk with a plant stem or branch.

Leaf-margin: the edge of a leaf.

Leaflet: one of the leaf-like parts of a compound leaf.

Leaf-stalk: the narrow vein-like attachment of a leaf to the stem or branch of the plant. Leaves of some species have no leaf-stalk.(See: Sessile)

Linear: descriptive of very narrow leaves with edges being more or less parallel.

Lip: an enlarged lower petal which may be a single petal or comprise two or more fused petals.

Lobe: indentation or projecting segment of the edge of a leaf or petal; often irregular in shape.

Marsh: a wetland area covered by moss, grass and other low growth; usually underlain by varying depths of decayed organic matter (peat) and may contain small areas of open water without visible source or outlet.

Mat: a dense carpet of growth, sometimes formed by prolific growth of rootstock; sometimes by very slow growth and expansion of low, creeping plants over surprisingly long periods of time.

Mid-rib: the main vein extending along the centre of a leaf or leaflet.

Monocotyledon: the occurrence of only one "seed-leaf" at the initial stage of plant growth (germination). This characteristic destinguishes one of the two main groups of flowering plants. (see "dicotyledon")

Monoecious: the term applied to the characteristic of those species which bear male and female flowers separately on the same plant.

Mycorrhiza: the mutually beneficial association between plants and soil fungus whereby soil fungus receives surplus sugar from plants and supplies phosphate to plants in return.

Naturalized: being well established and growing wild in an area, but originating from another region or part of the world.

Nectary: any organ or location on a plant where nectar is secreted.

Nerve: a term often applied to the main vein or ribs of a leaf, particularly the central vein or mid-rib.

Node: the location of specialized cells on the stem of a plant, sometimes visible as a swelling or

hardening, from which leaves, branches or roots may arise.

Ochrea: a tubular membrane occurring as a sheath around each node on the stem of plants of the Smartweed Family *(Polygonaceae).*

Ovary: the base of the 3-part female organ of a flower (pistil) containing female cells awaiting fertilization. In some flowers the ovary is located above the point of juncture of the petals, sepals and stamens (superior ovary). In others it is located below this juncture (inferior ovary).

Palate: refers to the upper surface of a petal or fused petals forming the lip of a lipped flower where it arches into the flower tube or "throat" containing the sexual parts.

Palmate: descriptive of a leaf having lobes or leaflets which radiate from a terminal point on the leaf-stalk as fingers from the hand.

Panicle: a branching cluster of separately stalked flowers.

Parasitic: being attached to and entirely dependent upon another living plant for food supply.

Part (Parted): a unit of one of the characteristic componants of a flower (petal, sepal or stamen).

Pendulent: occurring in a hanging or suspended position.

Petal: one of a group of protective structures of a flower, modified in colour, texture or shape to produce nectar or scent, attractive to insects needed for pollination.

Petiole: a leaf-stalk.

Photosynthesis: the process by which plants produce complex organic molecules from the action of light energy on chlorophyll, water and mineral ions contained in the water.

Pinnate: descriptive of compound leaves having paired or alternating leaflets arranged in two rows along a central vein or mid-rib. Bi-pinnate leaves have leaflets similarly arranged along secondary ribs, and tri-pinnate leaves have leaflets arising from tertiary ribs.

Pistil: the seed-forming portion of a flower which includes a stigma, style and ovary.

Plant: a unit of a species within the Plant Kingdom capable of maturity and reproduction.

Pod: a seed case that splits open on maturity to release the individual seeds contained therein.

Pollen: fine grain containing a male sex cell produced on stamen anthers. The form, size and surface design of pollen grains are unique to each species.

Pollination: the transfer of pollen from anther to stigma (by wind, insect or gravity). The sticky moistness on the surface of the stigma activates germination of the male cell from which a pollen tube grows and extends down the style to contact and fertilize one of the egg cells in the ovary.

Prickles: short, sharp outgrowths occuring on the stem, leaves, or both. They may be in the form of stiff, straight hairs serving a protective function; or rows of curved hooks along the stem for climbing support; or in a variety of other forms for other purposes.

Prostrate: growing along the ground.

Protandrous: descriptive of flowers in which stamens mature before styles, thus avoiding self-polination and increasing the probability of cross-pollination.

Protogynous: descriptive of flowers in which styles mature before stamens, thus avoiding self-pollination and increasing the probability of cross-pollination.

Raceme: an elongate flower cluster with flowers occurring along either side of an axial stalk. The lowest flowers mature first and the cluster tapers to a growing tip where new flowers are continuously formed.

Radical: an embrionic root projecting from the seed.

Ray-floret: one of several to many small flowers with petals modified to form a single, long, strap-like projection. Commonly occur around the perimeter of a central disc of "tube-florets" in flowerheads of the Composite/ Daisy Family.

Reclining: descriptive of flower stems which tend to bend downwards, but not to the extent of being prostrate.

Recurved: descriptive of petal tips and/or sepals which flare outwards.

Reflexed: descriptive of petal tips and/or sepals which are recurved to the extent of pointing backwards.

Revolute: descriptive of leaves which have the edges turned downwards or rolled towards the lower side.

Rhizome: the over-wintering underground portion of a stem, bearing buds from which new growth may arise and producing new roots in subsequent years.

Root: the part of a plant that grows into the soil, stabilizing the plant in place and serving to absorb and convey water and nutrients to the stem. In perennial plants the roots may also be modified for food storage during dormant periods.

Rootstock: enlarged main body of the root-system of perennial plants, modified to function as a food storage reservoir.

Rosette: a circle or series of circles of leaves arising from the base of a plant at the juncture of the stem and root.

Runner: a prostrate stem capable of rooting from nodes at which point new plants may grow and initiate new runners.

Sap: liquid nutrients transported by a plant's circulatory system.

Saprophytic: being dependent on decayed organic matter and a mycorrhizal association with soil fungus for food supply.

Scale: a thin cellular membrane in the form of a plate, flap or projection which may be specialized protective tissue or a rudimentary or degenerate leaf.

Scalloped: descriptive of leaf margins in the form of a series of rounded segments

Seed: the ripened result of fertilization, contained in a protective coat, and capable of eventual germination.

Sepal: one of a group of protective structures of a flower. Sepals occur in a ring immediately below the petals and sometimes in place of petals. They encase the flower when in bud and in those instances where a flower opens and closes in response to various stimuli.

Serrate: descriptive of the edge or margin of a leaf by formed of a series of sharply pointed, toothlike projections like the edge of a saw.

Sessile: descriptive of a flower or leaf connected directly to a stem, there being no flower- or leaf-stalk.

Sexual: pertaining to the method of reproduction by means of the fusion of specialized male and female cells.

Sheath: a thin protective structure wrapped around the juncture of a stem and stalk.

Shrub: a woody, branching plant, shorter than a tree.

Simple: broadly descriptive of any leaf that is not a compound leaf (variously comprised of leaflets), but may vary from being straight-edged to curved edge and to being variously lobed.

Smooth: the absence of hairs and prickles.

Solitary: descriptive, particularly of flowers occurring singly, not in groups or clusters.

Spathe: a large leaf-like or petal-like bract partly enfolding a flower cluster.

Spatulate: descriptive of a leaf having a broad, rounded end and narrowing towards the base.

Species: the basic unit of biological classification, each recognized unit being assigned a latinized second name in conjunction with its first (genus) name. All members of a species share broadly uniform characteristics and are capable of freely interbreeding.

Specimen: a plant or flower selected as being representative of its type.

Spike: specifically, a long raceme of unstalked flowers; but commonly and more broadly descriptive of any elongate floral cluster.

Spine: a stiff, sharp-pointed projection from a plant, usually longer and sturdier than prickles.

Spur: the modified portion of a petal or sepal forming a tubular projection, usually projecting to the rear of the flower.

Stalk: a term generally used interchangeably with "stem", but used more specifically in this text to refer only to the length of vegetative attachment between a stem and a flower or leaf.

Stamen: the male organ of a flower, consisting of a filament surmounted by a pollen-bearing anther, usually occurring severally or numerously in a ring around the base of the female organ.

Staminoid: an infertile stamen. Where these occur they are usually paired with fertile stamens.

Standard: the term applied either to the erect upper petal characteristic of some flowers of the Pea Family or to the three erect central petals of Irises.

Stem: a term generally used interchangeably with "stalk", but used more specifically in this text to refer only to the main axial structure of a plant.

Sterile: pertaining to infertility or non-production of pollen or seed.

Stigma: the variousely formed tip of the female organ of a flower (pistil) to which pollen grains adhere.

Stipule: a leaf-like growth occurring at the base of a leaf-stalk in some species of plants.

Style: the connecting structure between the stigma and the ovary.

Succulent: pertaining to the thick juicy fleshiness characteristic of the leaves or stem of some plants.

Symmetry: the balanced uniformity of appearance, characteristic of flowers, which in some are symmetrical around a central point, as a dandelion or daisy (radial symmetry); others, such as bellflowers, are symmetrical around a central axis (axial symmetry); still others, such as pea flowers and orchids, are symmetrical in relation to a central plane (bilateral symmetry).

Taproot: a relatively long and strong, downward-growing branch of a root system.

Tendril: a long slender outgrowth produced from the stem or leaves of some plants, which, by coiling around other objects, assist the plant to climb and maintain stability.

Terminal: located at the extreme end of a stem, branch or stalk.

Thorn: a stiff sharp-pointed projection from a woody plant, similar to a spine.

Toothed: descriptive of sharply pointed indentations and projections occurring in series along the edge or margin of a leaf.

Trailing: descriptive of stems which bend or arch outwards and are so flexible or weakly constructed in their extremity that they hang vertically downwards to or towards the ground.

Tri-pinnate: (see: pinnate)

Tube-floret: one of the several to many small, tube-shaped flowers which make up the central disc of a flowerhead in the Composite/Daisy Family.

Tuft: a low-growing tightly bunched group of stems.

Umbel: a flower cluster in which flower-stalks all arise from a single point.

Variable: descriptive of highly adaptive plant species which may alter their appearance from one area to another, sometimes to an extent making recognition difficult.

Variety: a plant which differs in one or more characteristic from others of the same species.

Vegetative reproduction: the formation of new plants from a parent plant without recourse to the fusion of male and female sex cells. Asexual reproduction resulting in "clones" of the parent, as occurs in the formation of bulbils.

Vein (Venation): the structural lines of a leaf through which water and nutrients are transported.

Vestigial: small or degenerate organ or part.

Vine: a climbing woody-stemmed plant.

Weed: a derogatory term applied to a plant growing where it is not wanted, but often used in reference to any uncultivated plant.

Whorl: three or more leaves or flowers arising from the same cross-sectional location on a stem.

Index of Common Names

89

90

Index of Scientific Names

Achillea ptarmica 65,66
  millefolium 66
Aconitum napellus 10
Agrimonia striata 21
Ajuga reptans 47
Alchemilla vulgaris 21
Alisma 73
Alismataceae 73
Alopecurus pratensis 1
Amelanchier 17
Anaphalis margaritacea 66
Andromeda glaucophylla 38
Anemone nemorosa 9
  parviflora 9
Angelica atropurpurea 33
Antennaria spathulata 66
Anthemis arvensis 64
  cotula 64
Anthriscus sylvestris 33
Apiaceae 32
Apocynaceae 42
Apocynum androsaemifolium 42
Aquilegia vulgaris 10
Arabis alpina 13
Aralia 34
  hispida 34
  nudicaulis 34
  racemosa 34
Araliaceae 34
Arctium minus 58
Arenaria groenlandica 6
  lateriflora 7
  peploides 7
Arethusa bulbosa 80
Armeria 41
  maritima 41, 42
Aronia prunifolia 17
Artemesia absinthium 72
  lactiflora 72
  vulgaris 72
Aster gracilis 67
  nemoralis 67
  novae-angliae 68
  novi-belgii 68
  puniceus 67
  radula 67, 71
  umbellatus 67
Asteraceae 57, 55
Atriplex 5
  patula 5
Atropa belladonna 48
Balsaminaceae 26
Barbarea vulgaris 13, 4
Bartsia alpina 49
Betula michauxii 67, 71
Bellis perennis 65
Bidens frondosa 68, 2
Boraginaceae 45

Brassica juncea 13
  napus 13
Cakile edentula 12, 45
Calluna vulgaris 37
Calopogon tuberosus 80
Caltha palustris 9
Calystegia 43
  sepium 43
Campanula rapunculoides 55
  rotundifolia 56
Campanulaceae 55
Caprifoliaceae 54
Capsella bursa-pastoris 11
Cardamine pensylvanica 14
  pratensis 14
Carum carvi 33
Caryophyllaceae 6
Cassiope tetragona 39
Castilleja 48
  septentrionalis 49
Centaurea cyanus 58
  nigra 58, 8
Cerastium alpinum 6
  beeringianum 6
  vulgatum 6
Chamaedaphne calyculata 38
Chamomilla suaveolens 59
Chelone glabra 49
Chenopodiaceae 4
Chenopodium album 5
  glaucum 5
  lanceolatum 5
Chrysanthemum leucanthemum 65
  parthenium 65
Circaea alpina 31
Cirsium arvense 57, 5
  muticum 57
  vulgare 57
Cladonia alpestris 37, 56
Clintonia borealis 74
Cochlearia groenlandica 13
Compositae 57, 55
Conioselinum chinense 32
Conringia orientalis 13
Convolvulaceae 43
Convolvulus 43
  sepium 43
Coptis groenlandica 9
Corallorhiza maculata 81
Cornaceae 31
Cornus canadensis 31
  stolonifera 31
  suicica 31
Coronilla varia 24
Crasulaceae 14
Crepis biennis 63
Cruciferae 11
Cypripedium acaule 79

Bibliography

Ayre, A. M., Newfoundland Flowers, The Book Of Newfoundland, Vol.1, Newfoundland Book Publishers Ltd., St. John's, 1937.

Fernald, M.L., Grey's Manual of Botany. Eighth Edition. American Book Company, New York, 1950. (Corrected printing, 1970).

Forey, P. Wild Flowers of North America, Dragon's World Ltd., Limpsfield, Surrey, 1990.

Fitter, A. and Attenborough, D. (Ed.), New Generation Guide to the Wildflowers of Britain and Northern Europe; William Collins Sons & Co. Ltd., London, W I, 1987.

Griffin, D., Barrett, W., MacKay, A., Atlantic Wildflowers, Oxford University Press, Toronto, Ont., 1984.

Macpherson, A.G. & Macpherson, J.B. (Editors), The Natural Environment of Newfoundland, Past and Present, Department of Geography, Memorial University of Newfoundland, 1981.

Meadus, W. J., Moores, L., Forest Site Classification Manual, FRDA Report 003, Canada, 1989.

Montgomery, F. H., Plants from Sea to Sea, The Ryerson Press, Toronto, Ontario, 1966.

Mulligan, G. A., Common Weeds of Canada, McClelland & Stewart Ltd., Canada, 1976.

Newfoundland Natural History Society, The Osprey, Vol. 3, No.1, 1977

Peterson, R. T. and McKenny, M., A Field Guide to Wildflowers of Northern and Northcentral North America, Houghton Mifflin Company, Boston, Mass., 1968.

Porsild, A. E., National Museum of Canada, Bul. 146.

Rouleau, E., Rouleau's List of Newfoundland Plants, Oxen Pond Botanic Park, St. John's, Newfoundland. 1978.

Ryan, A. G., Native Trees and Shrubs of Newfoundland and Labrador, Parks Division, Department of Environment and Lands, Government of Newfoundland and Labrador, St. John's, NF, 1978.

Smallwood, Joseph R.(Editor in Chief), Encyclopedia of Newfoundland and Labrador, Vols. 1 & 2, Newfoundland Book Publishers (1967) Ltd., St. John's, NF, 1981 1985.

Smallwood, Joseph R. - Heritage Foundation Inc,, Encyclopedia of Newfoundland and Labrador, Vols. 3,4 & 5, Harry Cuff Publications Ltd., St. John's, NF, 1991, 1993, 1994.

Terry, H., A Victorian Flower Album, The Viking Press, New York, 1978.

Flower Locations by Region

Nain ┃7-1

L A B R A D O R

NEWFOUNDLAND

Flower Locations: Labrador Region

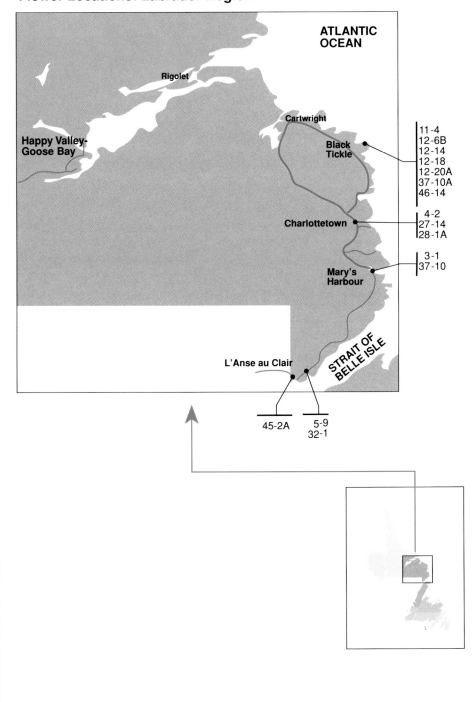

Flower Locations: Great Northern Region

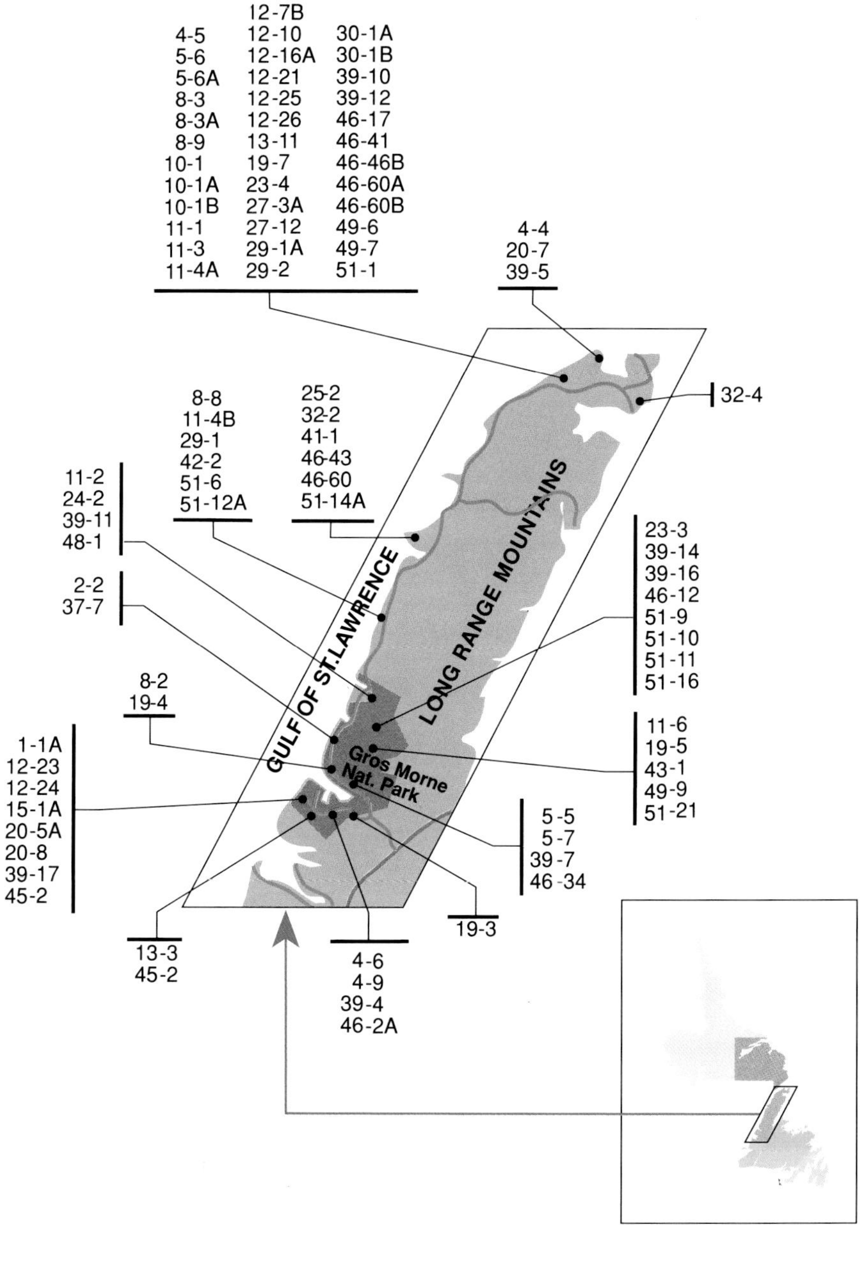

```
        12-7B
4-5     12-10    30-1A
5-6     12-16A   30-1B
5-6A    12-21    39-10
8-3     12-25    39-12
8-3A    12-26    46-17
8-9     13-11    46-41
10-1    19-7     46-46B
10-1A   23-4     46-60A
10-1B   27-3A    46-60B
11-1    27-12    49-6
11-3    29-1A    49-7
11-4A   29-2     51-1
```

```
4-4
20-7
39-5
```

```
8-8      25-2
11-4B    32-2
29-1     41-1
42-2     46-43
51-6     46-60
51-12A   51-14A
```

```
32-4
```

```
11-2
24-2
39-11
48-1
```

```
2-2
37-7
```

```
23-3
39-14
39-16
46-12
51-9
51-10
51-11
51-16
```

GULF OF ST. LAWRENCE

LONG RANGE MOUNTAINS

```
8-2
19-4
```

```
11-6
19-5
43-1
49-9
51-21
```

```
1-1A
12-23
12-24
15-1A
20-5A
20-8
39-17
45-2
```

Gros Morne Nat. Park

```
5-5
5-7
39-7
46-34
```

```
19-3
```

```
13-3
45-2
```

```
4-6
4-9
39-4
46-2A
```

Flower Locations: South Western Region

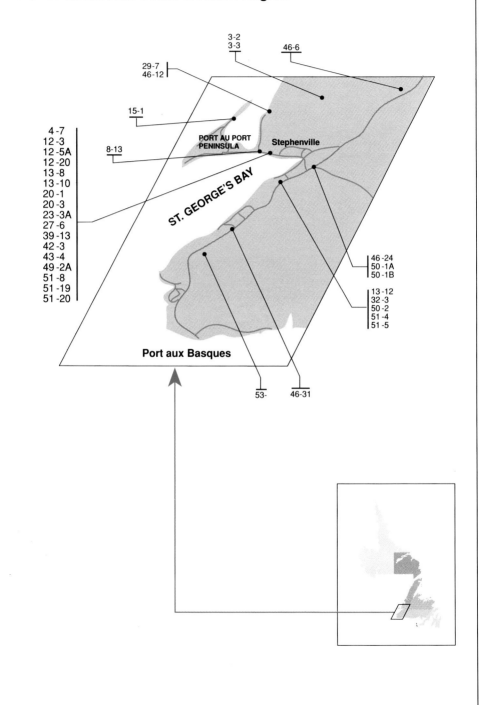

3-2
3-3

46-6

29-7
46-12

15-1

4 -7
12 -3
12 -5A
12 -20
13 -8
13 -10
20 -1
20 -3
23 -3A
27 -6
39 -13
42 -3
43 -4
49 -2A
51 -8
51 -19
51 -20

8-13

PORT AU PORT
PENINSULA

Stephenville

ST. GEORGE'S BAY

46 -24
50 -1A
50 -1B

13 -12
32 -3
50 -2
51 -4
51 -5

Port aux Basques

53-   46-31

Flower Locations: North Eastern Region

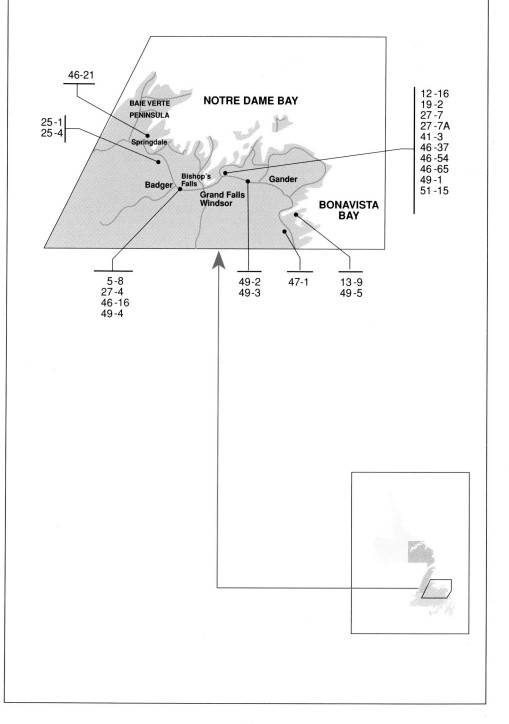

46-21

25-1
25-4

BAIE VERTE
PENINSULA

NOTRE DAME BAY

Springdale

Bishop's
Falls

Badger

Grand Falls
Windsor

Gander

**BONAVISTA
BAY**

12-16
19-2
27-7
27-7A
41-3
46-37
46-54
46-65
49-1
51-15

5-8
27-4
46-16
49-4

49-2
49-3

47-1

13-9
49-5

Flower Locations:Avalon Region

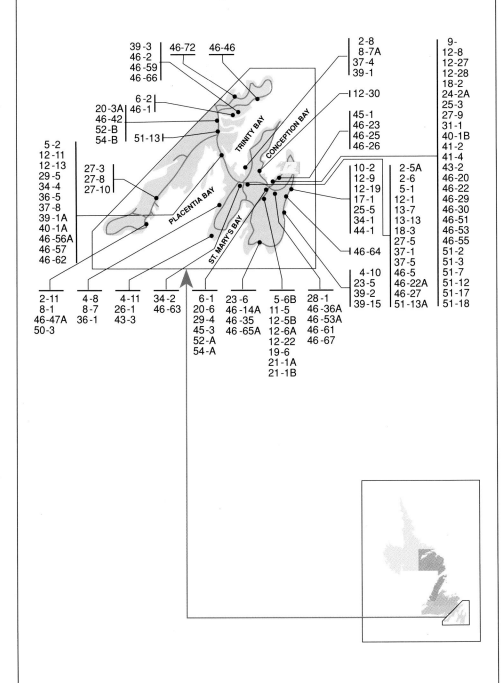

39-3
46-2
46-59
46-66

46-72   46-46

6-2
20-3A 46-1
46-42
52-B
54-B   51-13

5-2
12-11
12-13
29-5
34-4
36-5
37-8
39-1A
40-1A
46-56A
46-57
46-62

27-3
27-8
27-10

TRINITY BAY

CONCEPTION BAY

PLACENTIA BAY

ST. MARY'S BAY

2-8
8-7A
37-4
39-1

12-30

45-1
46-23
46-25
46-26

10-2   2-5A
12-9   2-6
12-19   5-1
17-1   12-1
25-5   13-7
34-1   13-13
44-1   18-3
        27-5
46-64   37-1
        37-5
4-10   46-5
23-5   46-22A
39-2   46-27
39-15   51-13A

9-
12-8
12-27
12-28
18-2
24-2A
25-3
27-9
31-1
40-1B
41-2
41-4
43-2
46-20
46-22
46-29
46-30
46-51
46-53
46-55
51-2
51-3
51-7
51-12
51-17
51-18

2-11   4-8   4-11   34-2   6-1   23-6   5-6B   28-1
8-1   8-7   26-1   46-63   20-6   46-14A   11-5   46-36A
46-47A 36-1   43-3   29-4   46-35   12-5B   46-53A
50-3   45-3   46-65A   12-6A   46-61
                                52-A   12-22   46-67
                                54-A   19-6
                                                 21-1A
                                                 21-1B

104

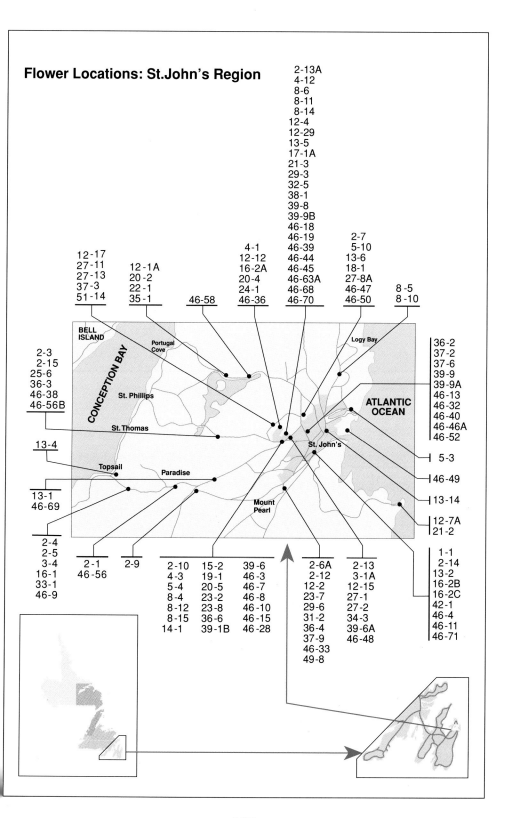

Flower Locations: St.John's Region

Prints of photographs

contained in this book

may be obtained from

Flora Frames
P.O. Box 28141,
St. John's, NF Canada
A1B 4J8